BLACK AMERICANS:
ISSUES AND CONCERNS

BLACK AMERICANS: ISSUES AND CONCERNS

Edited by
N. N. Rachveli

Nova Science Publishers, Inc.

Art Director: Christopher Concannon
Graphics: Elenor Kallberg and Maria Ester Hawrys
Manuscript Coordinator: Roseann Pena
Book Production: Tammy Sauter, and Michelle Lalo
Circulation: Irene Kwartiroff and Annette Hellinger

Library of Congress Cataloging-in-Publication Data

Black Americans : issues and concerns /
N. N. Rachveli, editor.
p. cm.
Includes bibliographical references (p.) and index.
ISBN 1-56072-173-1 : $59.00
1. Afro-Americans--Social conditions--1975- .
I. Rachveli, N. N.
E185.86.B5239 1994 94-1779
305.896'073--dc20 CIP

6080 Jericho Turnpike, Suite 207
Commack, New York 11725
Tele. 516-499-3103 Fax 516-499-3146
E Mail Novasci1@aol.com

Printed in the United States of America

CONTENTS

BLACK AMERICANS: SELECTED ISSUES

G.P. Laney

FEDERAL RESEARCH AND DEVELOPMENT FUNDING AT HISTORICALLY BLACK COLLEGES AND UNIVERSITIES

C.M. Matthews

THE VOTING RIGHTS ACT OF 1965, AS AMENDED: ITS HISTORY AND CURRENT ISSUES

G.P. Laney

RACE ISSUES IN THE UNITED STATES BASED ON NATIONAL PUBLIC OPINION POLLS

M.A. Aubin

ISBN 1-56072-173-1

BLACK AMERICANS: SELECTED ISSUES*

G.P. Laney

MOST RECENT DEVELOPMENTS

President Clinton's budget included proposals that address special needs of, or have particular impact on, many issues before the black community. These issues encompass education, tax and income support policies, social service programs, health care reform, environmental hazards concerns, crime and drug problems, and foreign affairs.

The presidential budget expands the Earned Income Tax Credit (EITC). Senator Moynihan and Representative Rostenkowski, at the Administration's request, introduced bills, S. 876 and H.R. 1960, respectively, that include the President's proposed changes to the EITC.

Several bills promoting environmental justice have been introduced in the 103rd Congress. A recently passed Senate bill, S. 171, requires the Environmental Protection Agency to maintain an Office of Environmental Justice.

BACKGROUND AND ANALYSIS

This issue brief summarizes and analyzes selected legislative issues before the 103rd Congress of special interest to the black community. (Throughout this brief, the terms African-American and black are used synonymously.) The issues were chosen because of their disproportionate impact on, or because of an identified need within, the African-American community. Each topic within a subject area offers a brief background on the issue, tells why Congress is addressing the issue, identifies legislation where appropriate, and refers readers to other CRS products for a more comprehensive treatment of the subject.

* Excerpted from CIS Issue Brief IB93059 and IB92070

Education

Two primary issues in education considered by the 102d Congress were of particular importance for black Americans: providing access to higher education and improving elementary and secondary education.

Access to Higher Education

Access to higher education by black Americans has been a long-standing Federal concern. Many Federal higher education programs seek to promote equal educational opportunity. Further, concern has been raised recently that the Nation will not meet its economic and scientific challenges unless greater numbers of minorities and women enter mathematical and scientific fields.

The *number* of African-American men and women enrolled in higher education and African-American enrollment *rates* offer a mixed picture of current higher education access. The *number* of black Americans enrolled today is higher than in the mid-1970s. Enrollment by African-American women has steadily increased; enrollment by African-American men fell until the mid-1980s, but has grown significantly since. While higher education enrollment *rates* of young African-American high school graduates have been relatively stable, rates for whites have increased, widening the gap between these two groups.

The 102d Congress approved legislation (P.L. 102-325, Higher Education Amendments of 1992) reauthorizing the Higher Education Act (HEA), the source of many programs of importance to African-American access to higher education. The HEA authorizes multi-billion dollar programs of primarily undergraduate financial assistance for low-income students; assistance for minorities to pursue graduate and professional education; support for historically black colleges and other institutions serving minorities and the disadvantaged; and programs providing services to low-income students to enable them to finish high school and pursue higher education. Over half of African-American undergraduates receive Federal student assistance; less than a third of white undergraduates are so aided.

Public Law 102-325 authorizes increases in the amount of aid for low-income and minority students while also expanding eligibility for, and aid to, moderate-income students. Among the new initiatives important to African-Americans are early intervention programs providing disadvantaged elementary and secondary students with support services and a guarantee of higher education financial assistance; significant increases in the size of the needs-tested Pell Grants for undergraduate education; and changes to facilitate application for financial aid by the poorest students.

In a related issue, the U.S. Department of Education is attempting to clarify the circumstances under which higher education institutions may offer student financial assistance programs restricted to minority students. This move has prompted concern among some observers that the amount of financial aid focused on minority students, including black Americans, will be reduced.

Improvement of Elementary and Secondary Education

For nearly a decade, education and government policymakers have sought to reform U.S. elementary and secondary education for various reasons. Some efforts have been sparked by a belief that eroding U.S. international economic competitiveness is a product of declining achievement by U.S. students. Some arise from concern that certain groups of students, such as black Americans, who constitute a growing segment of school-age population, disproportionately experience academic failure.

President Bush and the Nation's governors adopted six National Education Goals that call for improvement in the educational performance of **all** students. The President proposed AMERICA 2000, a series of actions to achieve the Goals (H.R. 2460; S. 1141). Among the principal components of this strategy were school choice, new model schools, national education standards, and a national system of assessments to measure progress toward the standards. Questions have been raised about the impact of these proposals on minority and low-income students, with some critics asserting that the strategy generally overlooks the special needs of disadvantaged pupils.

The 102d Congress developed legislation (S. 2) that included alternatives to some of the President's reform approaches. Proposed alternatives included systemic reform that would have committed entire statewide school systems to higher educational outcomes for all students through coordinated activities such as goal setting, teacher development and assessment, and holding schools accountable for student achievement. Special financial assistance targeted to schools serving pupils with greater educational needs, many of whom are likely to be minority students, was also considered. The conference version of S. 2 failed to be enacted.

Improving elementary and secondary teaching has also become a focus of education reform. Concerned that a small and declining portion of precollegiate teachers are African-American or other minorities, the 102d Congress included in the HEA reauthorization bill programs to attract individuals from these groups to teaching.

For a decade, policymakers have sought to improve U.S. elementary and secondary education for various reasons. Foremost among them are a belief that declining academic achievement of U.S. students threatens U.S. international economic competitiveness; and concern that certain groups of low-income and minority students, such as African-Americans, disproportionately experience academic failure.

In 1990, President Bush and the Nation's Governors adopted six National Education Goals calling for improvement in the educational performance of **all** students. Although the 101st and 102nd Congresses debated bills supporting steps toward achievement of the National Education Goals, these bills did not become law. (CRS Report 92-884 EPW, *National Education Goals and Federal Policy Issues: Action by the 102nd Congress.*) The 103rd Congress has already begun to revisit issues surrounding educational improvement and the National Education Goals. The Clinton Administration will seek passage of legislation similar to the Neighborhood Schools Improvement Act considered by the 102nd Congress. According to Secretary of Education Riley, this legislation will support national and statewide systemic reform of education by, among other provisions, codifying the Goals; establishing a council to certify national standards for curriculum content and national assessments measuring progress toward the Goals; creating a council for development of voluntary, national standards to gauge school systems' educational capacity ("opportunity to learn"); providing Federal assistance to States and school districts with "action strategies" to achieve the National Education Goals; and reducing Federal rules and regulations accompanying education funding.

During debate on such proposals in the 102nd Congress, critics asserted that these reforms generally overlook the special needs of minority and low-income pupils and the severe disparities in the educational opportunities afforded them. Further, they posited that national assessments will place disadvantaged students at increased risk for academic failure if they are used for "high stakes" purposes (e.g., determining graduation from high school) **before** students have had an opportunity to master a curriculum based on new standards. Proponents counter that holding **all** students to high standards will prevent school systems from ignoring the needs of disadvantaged students. In addition, it is suggested that opportunity to learn standards will be used to identify basic resource inequities that should be addressed.

In addition, the 103rd Congress is expected to amend and extend the Elementary and Secondary Education Act (ESEA), whose legislative authority is expiring. ESEA currently supports programs central to Federal efforts to improve education and enhance the educational opportunities of minority and low-income students. Among these programs are the multi-billion dollar Chapter 1 program of compensatory education for disadvantaged students; the Magnet Schools Assistance program supporting special educational arrangements in desegregating school districts; and the Bilingual Education Act, designed to help students with limited English proficiency learn English. Debate will focus partly on how these and other ESEA programs can and should support broad State and Federal reform initiatives. Further, the impact of changes to these programs on services for minority and low-income students will be considered.

The 103rd Congress will also debate proposals to establish youth apprenticeship programs that link school-based academic instruction and work experience, and create work skills standards. (CRS Report 92-960 EPW, *Youth Apprenticeships: Improving School-to-Work Transition for the "Forgotten Half."*) These initiatives are supported by the Clinton Administration. Such proposals may increase the likelihood that minority and low-income students will complete high school and acquire the skills needed to enter the work force. Concerns may be raised about the extent to which participating students are steered away from college preparation and enrollment, with the possibility that some students' access to white-collar jobs will be restricted.

Higher Education Access and Progress

Minority access to, and progress in, higher education has been a long-standing Federal concern. Concern has been raised recently that the Nation will not meet its economic and scientific challenges unless more minorities and women enter mathematical and scientific fields.

The 102nd Congress extended the Higher Education Act (HEA), which authorizes many programs important for providing higher educational opportunities to minorities. These include multi-billion dollar programs of undergraduate financial assistance for low-income students; assistance for minorities to pursue graduate and professional education; support for historically black colleges and other institutions serving minorities and the disadvantaged; and programs providing support services to low-income students to enable them to finish high school and pursue higher education.

Also, the U.S. Department of Education (ED), beginning in 1990, sought to define the circumstances under which higher education institutions may offer financial assistance programs restricted to minorities. This effort has prompted concern by some that the amount of financial aid focused on minority students could be reduced.

Labor Issues

Labor Markets

Unemployment

As the 102d Congress came to a close, unemployment generally was still high and joblessness for black workers was worse than it has been in months. For October 1992, although the national jobless rate had decreased by four-tenths of one percent since June's highest rate in eight years of 7.8%, the reduction was attributed to a shrinkage in the labor force rather than an improvement in overall labor market conditions. In fact, unemployment among black workers was 13.9%, with the male adults in this group suffering 13.7%, more than twice the rate for white workers. For black teenagers, the statistics were even more grim: 42.5% for all black workers 16 to 19 years of age, and higher (44.2%) for the black teen-age male population, while young female teenagers were almost equally as bad off at 40.4%.

From a State-by-State perspective, those with high populations of black workers were among the ones with the highest unemployment rates. In October 1992, only 3 of the 11 largest States had unemployment rates less than the national average of 7.4%. Among the 11, California stood at 9.8%, New York at 8.7%, and Michigan at 8.6%. As the 102d Congress adjourned, bills containing major job-generating programs were left unresolved, including an infrastructure improvement program and the enterprize zone legislation, issues likely to be raised in the next Congress.

U.S. Labor Markets and Changing Foreign Economies

With trade negotiations between the U.S. and its trading partners continuing into 1993, their impact on specific segments of the U.S. labor force should be part of the deliberation. Although the expanding free world market can enhance corporate operations, the attraction of newly established large open foreign economies and the potential for increasing U.S. foreign direct investments in these nations can cause major disruptions in U.S. labor markets with serious consequences for large groups of black workers. In fact, although it has been receding as a proportion of the total labor force, U.S. manufacturing employment still provides jobs for 19 million American workers, many of whom are black. So the threat of a further, and possibly accelerated, downsizing of our manufacturing base can cause disproportionate job displacements for black male and female workers whose ratios of employment in manufacturing occupations are about twice as high as they are for white workers. Thus, ongoing trade negotiations with trading partners generally are important, such as those with Mexico and the European Community, as well as with Asian countries, especially the Peoples' Republic of China, which is responsible for the largest portion of the U.S. trade deficit next to Japan. Such negotiations can be crucial to U.S. labor markets and particularly to those markets with high concentrations of black workers. For example, in and around 100 U.S. cities, manufacturing makes up 20 to 60% of all employment. If job creation programs for urban centers are to be successful, they should consider the role manufacturing plays in generating substantial incomes for large proportions of black workers and their families, most of whom reside in cities. And, when trade and investment agreements are to be set, the impact they might have on important segments of our labor force should be part of the debate.

Employment and Training

The Job Training Reform Amendments of 1992, which amend the Job Training Partnership Act (JTPA), were signed into law on Sept. 7, 1992 (P.L. 102-367). JTPA, first enacted in 1982, is the Nation's primary employment and training program for disadvantaged adults and youth. The amendments are intended to increase targeting to very disadvantaged individuals and to strengthen the fiscal integrity of JTPA programs.

Of persons leaving JTPA's program for disadvantaged adults and youth (Title II-A) in program year 1990, 33% were African-Americans compared to 25% of all persons eligible for the program. Of program participants, African-Americans are more likely to be poor. They are less likely to enter jobs after leaving the program and are more likely to receive a lower starting wage. For example, of the 184,800 African-Americans who left the Title II-A program in 1990, 54% received public assistance compared with 42% of non-African Americans, and 49% got jobs compared with 58% of other persons. The average hourly starting wage for these African-Americans was $5.18 compared with $5.69 for other persons.

For FY1992, $4,707.6 million was appropriated for programs authorized by JTPA, including a $500 million emergency supplemental appropriation for JTPA's summer youth program. This supplemental appropriation in response to the Los Angeles riots is for the summer of 1992 and is added to the $682.9 million appropriated in FY1991 for the summer of 1992. The JTPA amendments permit local service delivery areas, with the Governor's approval, to use up to 10% of the funds appropriated for the summer of 1992 to provide services to youth in program year 1992 (July 1, 1992 to June 30, 1993).

For FY1993, appropriations legislation for the Departments of Labor, Health and Human Services, and Education (P.L. 102-394) provides $4,158.3 million for JTPA programs. The conference report (H.Rept. 102-974) includes $20 million for new Job Corps Centers. This will fund four new centers and bring the total number of Job Corps Centers to 113. JTPA's Job Corps program (Title IV-B) provides education, training, and supportive services in a residential setting to economically disadvantaged youth ages 16-21. In the program year ending June 30, 1991 (PY1990), 52% of Job Corps participants were African-Americans.

Unemployment Among African-American Workers

While the national unemployment rate has been moving down from the high in June 1992 of 7.7% and joblessness among all African-American workers also declined in early 1993, the black unemployment rate in February (seasonally adjusted) remained at a historic level of more than twice that of white workers (13.1% for African-Americans vs. 6.1% for whites). When teenage (16 to 19 years of age) rates are compared, unemployment for African-American youths showed no improvement from twelve months earlier (38.0%, or more than two times the 16.8% for white teenagers). Finally, for the first time in years, the unemployment rate for female teenagers exceeded that for male youths in February 1993 (38.6% to 37.4%), signalling, perhaps, a new situation among African-American workers.

Manufacturing and the African-American Labor Force

With negotiations between the U.S. and its trading partners continuing (General Agreements on Tariffs and Trade (GATT)) and with the North American Free Trade Agreement (NAFTA) due to come up for consideration in the 103rd Congress, the impact of these two agreements on U.S. industries with high levels of African-American employees will likely be part of the deliberation. Although the expanding free world market can enhance corporate operations, the attractions set in foreign economies, especially those, like Mexico, with a large force of accessible and trainable low-wage workers, can increase the potential for transferring U.S. operations to these nations. For example, shifts of manufacturing facilities to Mexico could create serious disruptions in those U.S. labor markets employing large groups of African-Americans. In fact, although it has been receding as a proportion of the total labor force, U.S. manufacturing employment still provides jobs for 19 million American workers, of which a disproportionate share are African American. In 144 U.S. metropolitan areas, manufacturing generates from 20% to 60% of all earnings of inhabitants. And in 61 of 190 larger U.S. cities, African-Americans make up from 25% to 65% of inhabitants. Thus, the threat of a further reduction and possible downsizing of our manufacturing base could cause job displacements for black male and female workers, whose ratios of employment in manufacturing occupations are about twice as high as they are for white workers.

The Fair Labor Standards Act and African Americans

In early 1989, Congress amended the Fair Labor Standards Act to set a new Federal hourly minimum wage rate. The present hourly rate of $4.25 has been in effect since April 1991. If the minimum wage rate had been adjusted for inflation (using the Consumer Price Index) at regular intervals since Jan. 1, 1978, however, it would have been slightly more than $6.00 an hour in February 1993, i.e., $1.75 more than the current rate. Consequently, bills are expected to be introduced in the 103rd Congress to increase the minimum wage rate again and, in some proposals, to also index it to some measurement of inflation so that it maintains its purchasing power as prices in the economy rise. Since a larger proportion of African-Americans are paid the minimum wage than of white workers (11.0% for African-Americans vs. 9.0% for white workers), proposals for raising the minimum wage should be of interest to this segment of the U.S. workforce.

Income Support Policies

Tax Relief for Lower- and Middle-Income Families with Children

Tax proposals were considered to stimulate the economy and promote more fairness in the tax system. Among other features, some proposals would have changed child exemptions or tax credits to working families with children, established new refundable child credits, and increased the Earned Income Tax Credit (EITC) for workers with children and adjusted gross incomes below $22,370 in 1992. A tax bill (H.R. 11), vetoed by President Bush, would have simplified the EITC. Such proposals reflect a trend of increased use of the Federal income tax system to provide benefits to lower-income, working families with children.

The vast majority of black families with children have members with earnings and, thus, could be affected by recent proposals to change Federal income taxes. Earnings of these families, however, are smaller than those of many other groups. For example, in 1991, among black families with children, 95% of married-couple families and 68% of single female-headed families had one or more members who worked at some time during the year. Median family income of black married couples with children was $35,358, compared to $43,179 for white married-couple families. Most of this was from earnings. Among black married-couple families with children and a working family member, 12.7% were poor; 4.4% of such families in which a member worked full-time, year-round were poor. These rates were almost twice those of white families. Relatively large proportions of African-American families with children generally would be favored by tax proposals that help low-income families.

Programs that Reduce Poverty Among Single-Parent Families

Low income is associated with a host of social ills, including lack of access to adequate medical care, poor nutrition, lack of access to safe and affordable housing, poor schools, long and costly commuting to good jobs, even early death. The high incidence of poverty among African-Americans, and especially their children, puts the group at disproportionate risk of being subject to one or more of these problems. (See CRS Reports 91-355 EPW, *Progress Against Poverty in the U.S. (1959 to 1989)* and 92-696 EPW, *Recent Statistics on Poverty in the United States: 1991*). In 1991, 45.6% of black children were poor, compared to 39.8% of Hispanic children and 16.1% of white children. Contributing to this high incidence of poverty is the large share of black children who live in single female-headed households (55.5% in 1991, compared to 27.3% of Hispanic and 16.2% of white children). Consequently, a greater share of black children than children of other races is eligible for government needs-tested programs, although black children still represent a minority of the children who receive government aid.

The Family Support Act of 1988, P.L. 100-485, which was promoted as major reform of the program of Aid to Dependent Children Act, strengthened the concept of mutual obligation. The duty of the welfare parent to prepare for work (through education, training, or work experience activities such as the Job Opportunities and Basic Skills (JOBS) program) and to seek and accept a job. The duty of the AFDC agency is to provide the cash benefit, education, training, and work activities, and support services such as child care and medical coverage. (See CRS report 88-702 EPW, *The Family Support Act of 1988: How It Changes the Aid to Families with Dependent Children (AFDC) and Child Support Enforcement Programs.*) The Act also included provisions aimed at making noncustodial parents take financial responsibility for their children, by strengthening child support enforcement tools and establishing paternity measures.

Since JOBS began in 1989-1990, 2 years of record-breaking AFDC caseloads, sharp increases in Medicaid, and high unemployment have strained State budgets, led to some benefit cuts, and produced a difficult environment for the program. In response, the 102d Congress passed legislation to expand Federal funding for efforts to promote employability of mothers enrolled in the Aid to Families with Dependent Children (AFDC) program. However, these provisions were embedded in H.R. 11 (Revenue Act of 1992), a massive and controversial bill that was pocket-vetoed by President Bush on November 5, just after the election. Also killed by the veto of H.R. 11 were several changes in AFDC law aimed at encouraging savings and self-employment of recipients and authorization for a demonstration of a community works progress (public jobs) program. Signed into law was a free-standing bill (S. 1002) that makes it a Federal crime to willfully fail to pay overdue child support on behalf of a child in another State. Bills not acted upon by the 102d Congress included ones to alter the AFDC/Medicaid matching rate formula, set an AFDC benefit floor, set a time limit on AFDC eligibility, expand EITC, and convert the income tax exemption for a child into a refundable tax credit.

Many AFDC changes are occurring at the State level. In his State of the Union message, President Bush said he would make it easier for States to alter AFDC, and his Administration has since granted waivers to California, Maryland, Michigan, New Jersey, Oregon, Utah, and Wisconsin to allow Federal AFDC funds for program changes that seek varied goals. Among these goals are the promotion of work, schooling, preventive health care, and marriage; deterrence of repeat childbearing and of migration for higher benefits. As means to these ends, both financial penalties and rewards are to be tested.

Low income is often associated with a host of social ills, including lack of access to adequate medical care and to safe, affordable housing; poor nutrition; lower-quality schools; long and costly commuting to good jobs; and even early death. The high incidence of poverty among African-Americans, and especially their children, puts the group at disproportionate risk for these conditions. (See CRS Reports 91-355 EPW, *Progress Against Poverty in the U.S. (1959 to 1989)* and 92-696 EPW, *Recent Statistics on Poverty in the United States: 1991.*) In 1991, 45.6% of black children were poor, compared to 39.8% of Hispanic children and 16.1% of white children. Contributing to this high incidence of poverty is the large share of black children who live in single female-headed households (55.5% in 1991, compared to 27.3% of Hispanic and 16.2% of white children). Consequently, a greater share of black children than children of other races is eligible for Government needs-tested programs, although black children still represent a minority of the children who receive Government aid. In 1988, a monthly average of 32.9% of all blacks received aid from a major income-tested program, compared to 8% of whites and 22.1% of Hispanics.

The Family Support Act of 1988, P.L. 100-485, a major revision of the program of Aid to Families with Dependent Children (AFDC), strengthened the concept of mutual obligation. The duty of the welfare parent is to prepare for work (through education, training, or work experience activities such as the Job Opportunities and Basic Skills (JOBS) program) and to seek and accept a job. The duty of the AFDC agency is to provide the cash benefit, education, training, work activities, and support services such as child care and medical coverage. (See CRS Report 88-702 EPW, *The Family Support Act of 1988: How It Changes the Aid to Families with Dependent Children (AFDC) and Child Support Enforcement Programs.*) The Act also included provisions aimed at making noncustodial parents take financial responsibility for their children, by strengthening child support enforcement tools and establishing paternity measures.

Since JOBS began in 1989-1990, 3 years of record-breaking AFDC caseloads, sharp increases in Medicaid, and high unemployment have strained State budgets, led to some AFDC benefit cuts, and produced a difficult environment for the JOBS program. President Clinton's budget indicates that the Administration will propose a welfare reform plan later this year, and Secretary of Health and Human Services Donna Shalala has said the President's reforms will build on the 1988 Family Support Act, which he helped shape as chairman of the National Governors' Association. Senator Moynihan has introduced in the 103rd Congress S. 16, which would authorize full funding for the JOBS program (no State matching would be required for new funds). The 102nd Congress voted a lesser expansion for JOBS funding, but it was in the tax bill (H.R. 11, The Revenue Act of 1992) that was vetoed by President Bush.

An integral part of the President's plan "to end welfare as we know it" is placing a time limit on AFDC receipt. In his State of the Union Message, President Clinton said that for up to 2 years, he would "empower" AFDC parents, chiefly mothers, with schooling, training, and child care needed to "break the cycle of dependency." Thereafter, those who "can work" would be required to do so, either in a private job or in community service. The House Republican leadership has introduced a bill (H.R.

741) that would place a 2-year time limit on AFDC benefits. In addition, a bill (S. 239) authorizing grants for pilot community work projects for AFDC recipients, parents with overdue child support obligations, and others was introduced by Senator Boren (companion bill, H.R. 652 was introduced by Representative English). Similar legislation authorizing pilot community work projects was passed by the 102nd Congress, but it too was in the vetoed tax bill. President Clinton will attempt to end poverty for children with a full-time working parent by expanding the Earned Income Tax Credit, and his budget includes this proposal, at an estimated cost of $6.7 billion in FY1997; the FY1994-1997 cost is estimated at $19.9 billion. Senator Moynihan and Representative Rostenkowski, at the request of the Administration, have introduced bills, S. 876 and H.R. 1960, respectively, that include the President's proposed changes to the EITC.

The Clinton budget says that the Administration plans to strengthen the Child Support Enforcement program by

> streamlining paternity establishment; using the IRS to collect seriously delinquent child support; making sure that absent parents who can pay child support do; setting up a national registry to track down deadbeat parents; requiring employees to report child support obligations on IRS W-4 forms; and improving medical support for children.

Many AFDC changes are occurring at the State level. Both the Reagan and Bush Administrations encouraged State experiments in welfare, granting waivers from Federal rules to test program changes. Waivers approved by the Bush Administration include tests of AFDC program changes that seek varied goals. Among these goals are the promotion of work, schooling, preventive health care, and marriage; deterrence of repeat childbearing and of migration for higher benefits. To achieve these goals, States are testing the use of both financial penalties and rewards. President Clinton told the National Governors' Association on Feb. 12, 1993, that there were "many promising initiatives right now at the State and local level" and that he favored more welfare experimentation, as long as results were measured.

Social Services

Head Start

Since 1965, Head Start has provided comprehensive early childhood development, educational, health, nutritional, social, and other services to primarily low-income preschool children and their families. In FY1993 the program was appropriated $2.8 billion. The 103rd Congress will examine the program for two reasons. One reason is that President Clinton has requested $500 million for Head Start FY1993 summer programs as part of his economic stimulus package. The other is that the program's authority expires at the end of FY1994. One of the major questions concerning Head Start is whether the program has expanded too quickly in recent years at the expense of program quality. According to DHHS, in FY1992, 37% of the 621,078 children enrolled in the program were black.

Child Welfare

The 102nd Congress passed a major child welfare reform bill, which was pocket-vetoed by President Bush. Similar legislation has been introduced in the 103rd Congress (S. 596), and President Clinton has announced that he has directed Secretary Shalala to develop a child welfare reform initiative. Since the mid-to-late 1980s, the Nation's child welfare system has been considered in a state of crisis, due to rising reports of child abuse and neglect and the number of children entering foster care. Child welfare administrators generally point to the introduction of crack cocaine in the mid-1980s as the immediate -- but not sole -- cause of the current situation. Combined with such factors as poverty, homelessness, AIDS, and other forms of substance abuse, the crack epidemic has been a final straw for many vulnerable families. Of children in foster care in 1989 (the latest year for which data are available), more than 34% were black, according to the American Public Welfare Association.

The public child welfare system is currently considered to be in a state of crisis. Both the number of reported incidents of child abuse/neglect, and the number of children entering foster care have increased in recent years. This crisis has been attributed to a combination of societal problems, including increased substance abuse, poverty, and homelessness. According to the American Public Welfare Association, African-American children are disproportionately represented within the child welfare system -- constituting 37% of children in foster care and 39% of children awaiting adoptive placement at the end of 1988. Research presented at a May 1992 hearing of the House Ways and Means Subcommittee on Human Resources indicated that being abused or neglected as a child increases a person's risk for an arrest as a juvenile by 53%, as an adult by 38%, and for a violent crime by 38%. Abused or neglected African-American children had higher risks of being arrested than abused or neglected white children in this study.

Current child welfare issues include changing the financing structure of the major Federal programs that authorize funds in this area; increasing the amount of preventive services available for vulnerable families; alleviating financial stress on parents who adopt special needs children who later develop serious physical or emotional disabilities; and restructuring child protective service systems designed to investigate reports of child abuse and neglect.

On May 28, the President signed legislation that significantly amends and extends through FY1995 the Child Abuse Prevention and Treatment Act and three other Acts, which provide specific services to vulnerable families (P.L. 102-295). This law increases the authorization for the Child Abuse Act and three other Acts to a total of $329 million for FY1992. These four Acts received an appropriation of $110 million for FY1993. In addition, both the Senate (S.4) and House (H.R. 3603) passed major child welfare legislation in the 102d Congress. Components of both of these child welfare bills were included in the Omnibus Urban Aid Initiative (H.R. 11) and would have cost almost $2.2 billion. H.R. 11 was pocket-vetoed by President Bush.

Homelessness

Homelessness, once thought to be a temporary crisis, has proven to be an enduring problem. Research on homelessness has revealed that homeless people are both heterogeneous in their backgrounds and diverse in their life courses. Although no systematic and reliable data exist nationally on the demographics of the homeless population, estimates of the percentage of homeless people who are black range from 41% to 48%, a greater proportion than blacks are of the poverty population. The roots of homelessness can be traced to both the personal problems of individuals, such as substance abuse and mental illness, and to structural social and economic problems, such as unemployment and housing costs.

Several years ago, Congress responded to the problem of homelessness in America with the Stewart B. McKinney Homeless Assistance Act (P.L. 100-77). This Act established a wide range of programs and benefits for homeless people, including health care, emergency food and shelter, mental health services, transitional housing, education, and job training, to deal with the acute and varied circumstances that homeless people face. As the 102d Congress responded to requests by the Administration and many State officials to consolidate some of these programs, it debated funding levels. Several of the McKinney program authorizations, particularly the HUD homeless assistance programs and the FEMA Emergency Food and Shelter Program, were set to expire at the end of FY1992. Legislation to reauthorize these McKinney Act programs was enacted as part of H.R. 5334, the Housing and Community Development Act of 1990.

Employment and Training

Since 1982, the Job Training Partnership Act (JTPA) has been the Nation's primary employment and training program for disadvantaged adults and youth. Amendments passed in the 102nd Congress (P.L. 102-367) are intended to increase targeting to very disadvantaged individuals and to strengthen the fiscal integrity of JTPA programs. For FY1993, $4,233.3 million was appropriated for JTPA programs, including $20 million for new Job Corps Centers. The job corps program (Title IV-B) provides education, training, and supportive services in a residential setting to economically disadvantaged youths, aged 16-21. The Clinton Administration has proposed increasing the number of Job Corps participants from 70,000 to 104,000 by 2001.

The Administration has also requested $1 billion for an FY1993 supplemental appropriation for the summer youth employment and training program (Title II-B) as part of a "stimulus" package. The Administration proposes allocating about 47% of the all funds available for the program in the summer of 1993 to the 100 cities with the greatest number of eligible youth.

In the program year ending June 30, 1991, 52% of job corps participants were African Americans. In addition, of persons leaving JTPA's program for disadvantaged adults and youth (Title II-A) in program year 1991, 34% were African-Americans compared to 24% of all persons eligible for the program. Compared to other program participants, African-Americans are more likely to be poor, are less likely to enter jobs after leaving the program, and are more likely to receive a lower starting wage.

National Service

National service refers to requiring or allowing citizens to perform public service work, usually in exchange for benefits such as education assistance. President Clinton has stated that he will propose a new national service program in which up to 100,000 students could pay for college or other post-secondary education through community service. If fully implemented, the program would cost $7.4 billion over the next several years. The President has requested $15 million for the 1993 Summer of Service program, the initial component of his national service program, as part of his economic stimulus package.

The 103rd Congress will also consider extending two existing national and community service Acts whose funding authority expires at the end of FY1993 -- the Domestic Volunteer Service Act and the National and Community Service Act. One of the fastest growing national service programs is conservation and youths corps, which involves young people (often from disadvantaged backgrounds) working on projects such as cleaning rivers; approximately 40% of youths in these programs in 1992 were African American.

Crime and Drugs

During the past 30 years or so, opinion polls have consistently registered Americans' high degree of concern over the often intertwined problems of crime and the misuse of narcotics and other dangerous drugs. The apparent breakdown of law in parts of the Nation -- developing in tandem with spreading use of such drugs as heroin, cocaine, and marijuana -- has fueled a search for solutions at all levels of government. While drug abuse is not solely an aspect of the crime problem, but also a health and general culture issue, much of the effort to curb it has arguably been driven by alarm over rising crime rates.

The particular interest with which African-Americans and other minority-group members may view the crime problem derives from its sometimes disproportionate impact, in recent times, on such groups. From 1979 to 1986, the crime victimization rate was 44 per 1,000 blacks and 34 per 1,000 whites, a special Justice Department study found. Also, African-Americans are disproportionately represented in the prison population. Of special concern is the involvement of young black males with the criminal justice system: one study found that on any given day, almost one in four black men in the age group 20-29 is in prison, jail, on probation, or on parole.

Finally, although all indicators are not in agreement, some evidence suggests that drug misuse could be a particular hazard for certain segments of the African-American community. Recent data show a disproportionate number of blacks among individuals receiving emergency room treatment for drug-related problems. This might be interpreted, although not necessarily, as a sign of more chronic or high-risk use by African-Americans than by other groups.

The Federal role in crime control does not lend itself to a broad-brush description. In the sense that "crime" means such offenses as homicide, robbery, assault, and burglary, that role has been significant only in recent times. Much of it has to do with giving financial or technical assistance to States and localities, the jurisdictions with more direct responsibilities in these matters; or it may be of a symbolic nature, i.e., passing statutes or adopting policies in the hope that State or local governments will be led to follow suit, or that a cultural statement will be made.

Specifically, with respect to control of narcotics and other dangerous drugs, the Federal Government has gradually assumed a large part of the responsibility over the course of a century. The current anti-drug strategy relies on activities and programs in five general areas: (1) regulation, interdiction, and other forms of "enforcement;" (2) bilateral overseas assistance and participation in international control efforts; (3) education and other prevention; (4) treatment of drug dependency; and (5) related research.

During the 102d Congress, a continuing interest in budget levels for crime and drug control was accompanied by development of, and major action on, new omnibus crime and drug control legislation (H.R. 3371; S. 1241). A conference agreement (on H.R. 3371) was approved by the House but was blocked in the Senate. This bill was in the tradition of omnibus laws enacted in 1984, 1986, 1988, and 1990. It or a similar proposal is the likely focal point of the crime and drug issues during the next Congress.

During the past 30 years or so, opinion polls have consistently reflected Americans' high level of concern over the often intertwined problems of crime and the misuse of narcotics and other dangerous drugs. The apparent breakdown of law in parts of the Nation -- developing in tandem with the spread in use of such drugs as heroin and cocaine -- has fueled a search for solutions at all levels of government. Whereas drug abuse is not solely an aspect of the crime problem, being also a health and general culture issue, much of the effort to curb it has arguably been driven by alarm over rising crime rates.

The special interest with which African-Americans and other minority-group members may view the crime problem derives from its disproportionate impact, in some respects, on such groups. In recent years, more African-Americans than whites have been the victims of crime: in 1991, the victimization rate was 106 per 1,000 blacks and 91 per 1,000 whites. Also, African-Americans are disproportionately represented in the prison population. Of special concern is the involvement of young black males with the criminal justice system: one study found that on any given day, almost one in four black men in the age group 20-29 is in prison, jail, on probation, or on parole.

Finally, although all indicators are not in agreement, some evidence suggests that drug misuse could be a particular hazard for certain segments of the African-American community. Recent data show a disproportionate number of blacks among individuals receiving emergency room treatment for drug-related problems. This might be interpreted, although not necessarily, as a sign of more chronic or high-risk use by African-Americans than by other groups.

The Federal role in crime control does not lend itself to a broad-brush description. In the sense that "crime" means such offenses as homicide, robbery, assault, and burglary, that role has been significant only in recent times. Much of it has to do with giving financial or technical assistance to States and localities, the jurisdictions with more direct responsibilities in these matters; or it may be of a symbolic nature, i.e., passing statutes or adopting policies in the hope that State or local governments will follow suit.

With respect to control of narcotics and other dangerous drugs, by contrast, the Federal Government has gradually assumed a large part of the responsibility over the course of a century. The current anti-drug strategy relies on activities and programs in five general areas: (1) regulation, interdiction, and other forms of "enforcement"; (2) bilateral overseas assistance and participation in international control efforts; (3) education and other prevention; (4) treatment of drug dependency; and (5) related research.

In the 103rd Congress, a continuing interest in budget levels and allocation ratios for crime and drug control is anticipated, as well as reconsideration of the omnibus crime, drug, and gun control legislation developed, but not enacted, during the 102nd Congress (H.R. 3371). This bill follows the tradition of omnibus laws enacted in 1984, 1986, 1988, and 1990.

Health

Life Expectancy

The health of African-Americans ranks behind that of American whites. Current morbidity and mortality rates for African-Americans are at levels last observed in white Americans decades ago. In 1988, life expectancy at birth was 69.5 years for African-Americans (the level achieved for whites in the 1950s) compared to 75.5 years for whites. Moreover, life expectancy at birth for African-American males was 64.9 compared to 72.3 for white males, and 73.4 for African-American females compared to 78.9 for white females. Even more alarming is the prominent rate of mortality for young African-American males due to HIV infection, to homicide, and to legal intervention (associated with law enforcement). They are the principal causes of death in such individuals age 15 to 44. The rate of homicide and legal intervention deaths in this group outnumbered those of whites in 1988 by a factor of 8 to 1 (289.1 compared to 35.1 per 100,000 individuals).

In addition to homicide, other major contributors to the life expectancy disparity among African-Americans and whites include cardiovascular diseases (e.g., heart disease and stroke), cancer, and infant mortality. Cardiovascular diseases, the number one cause of death in all races, killed 139.3 thousand African-Americans in 1988. Hypertension, a significant risk factor for both heart disease and stroke, is 1.5 to 1.7 times as prevalent in African-Americans as in white Americans. The infant mortality rate in the United States in 1988 was 10 deaths for every 1,000 live births, which is higher than virtually every other industrialized country. The infant mortality rate disparity among African-Americans and American whites is 17.6 for every 1,000 live births compared to 8.5. Among African-Americans, the infant mortality rate is higher than in many undeveloped countries. A key responsible factor for infant mortality that accounts for three-fourths of perinatal (the period shortly before and after birth) mortality and morbidity is prematurity. Prematurity is associated with poverty and unplanned pregnancies, which occur at significant levels in African-American females.

Legislation passed in the 102d Congress addressed a broad spectrum of health needs of African-Americans. Included was legislation that supported a number of preventive health and health services programs (H.R. 3635; P.L. 102-531).

Acquired Immune Deficiency Syndrome (AIDS)

According to the Centers for Disease Control, African-Americans are about two times as likely to suffer from Acquired Immune Deficiency Syndrome (AIDS) as whites. Minority women are even more likely to contract AIDS than white females. While African-Americans represent 12% of the total U.S. population, they constitute 29% of adult and adolescent AIDS cases and 54% of pediatric AIDS cases. The proportion of AIDS cases in African-Americans has been rising; in 1989, 27% of all persons with AIDS were black, currently the number is 29%. Among black men with AIDS, 43% acquired the disease through having sex with other men, and 36% through the use of intravenous drugs. In white men with AIDS, the comparable statistics are 79% and 7%. Among black women, 54% acquired AIDS through intravenous drug use and 36% through heterosexual contact; about 58% of the heterosexual contact cases had sex with an intravenous drug user.

Health Care

Health insurance coverage is an important factor in the ability to obtain health care services. In the United States, an estimated 34.6 million people have no health insurance and are not covered by the Medicaid program. Although Federal funds support Medicaid and other health programs that serve large numbers of racial and ethnic minorities, 21% of the non-elderly African-American population (compared to 12% of the non-elderly white population) have no health insurance. The uninsured are less likely than insured persons to obtain adequate health care. They are more likely to delay seeking care and to use emergency rooms for basic services. When they do get care, the uninsured are likely to be sicker and to need more costly treatment than the insured population. No doubt, the relative lack of access to health services contributes to African-Americans' documented disparities in health status.

Congress is addressing the health care access issue through various proposals to extend health insurance coverage. The proposals include providing tax incentives to purchase private coverage; mandating employers to provide coverage for employees and their dependents; instituting a national health insurance system; and expanding Medicaid.

Health Care Reform

Congress is considering a wide range of options for expanding access to, and reducing the costs of, health care. This attention to health care reform has been prompted by the large and growing number of Americans who lack health insurance and the rapid increase in health care spending.

In 1991, over 35 million Americans had no health insurance coverage. African-Americans are overrepresented among the uninsured. Compared to 14.7% of the white non-elderly population, 22.4% of black Americans under age 65 had no health insurance. (Most elderly Americans are covered by Medicare.)

Health care spending is increasing dramatically, rising from 10.9% of the gross domestic product (GDP) in 1988 to 14% of GDP, $832 billion, in 1992. Spending for health care is projected to grow to $1.6 trillion, 19% of GDP by the year 2000.

Numerous proposals address these problems, but little consensus exists on solutions. Some favor comprehensive health care reform to provide universal coverage and control costs. Three broad approaches to universal coverage would (1) build on the current employment-based system under which most people now obtain health insurance coverage, (2) establish a "single payer" system under which Government (Federal, State, or Federal/State partnership) sponsors and pays for care, or (3) expand an existing Federal program such as Medicare or Medicaid.

Some would modify the health care system through incremental steps such as (1) modification of tax laws to encourage the purchase of health insurance by individuals, or the provision of group health plans by employers, (2) promotion of health insurance purchasing groups through which small employers can join together to buy insurance, or (3) Federal preemption of State laws which require that insurance policies include certain benefits alleged to increase the price of insurance.

A presidential task force is scheduled to develop a health care reform proposal. Preliminary reports are that the President's proposal will include an employment-based approach and "managed competition" under which consumers would choose from a variety of competing health plans and would be given financial incentives to select the most cost-effective.

Different approaches have different effects on various groups. For example, some businesses and individuals may find that health insurance coverage is unaffordable even with tax credits and subsidies. Residents of some rural and inner city areas may find a dearth of competing health plans from which to choose. People with certain health conditions may find that no insurer will cover their particular health needs at any price.

Some lawmakers recommend that health care reform include expansion of programs that provide direct health services. Accordingly, there are proposals to expand federally funded health centers that provide free services to the very poor and charge others according to income and family size. These centers, however, focus on primary and preventive care and have limited resources for providing specialty care.

Environment

Several recent studies have revealed that black Americans and other racial minorities may be exposed to more pollution and bear greater health risks than whites due to the poor quality of their environment. Although the level of exposure to toxic substances also is related to income level, income alone does not seem to account for the uneven distribution of environmental hazards. For example, in families with annual incomes of less than $6,000, 68% of African-American children suffer high blood-lead levels, but only 36% of white children are similarly afflicted.

To assess the extent and severity of environmental inequities, the Environmental Protection Agency organized the Environmental Equity Workgroup in 1990. In its final report, released July 22, 1992, the Workgroup concluded:

> There are clear differences between racial groups in terms of disease and death rates. There are also limited data to explain the environmental contribution to these differences ... Racial minority and low-income populations experience higher than average exposures to selected air pollutants, hazardous waste facilities, contaminated fish and agricultural pesticides in the workplace ... A significantly higher percentage of black children compared to white children have unacceptably high blood lead levels.

EPA has established an Environmental Equity Office that will oversee and coordinate implementation of recommendations made by the Workgroup.EPA has established an Environmental Equity Office that will oversee and coordinate implementation of recommendations made by the Workgroup.

The Environmental Justice Act (H.R. 5326/S.2806) proposed to establish an EPA program to ensure nondiscriminatory compliance with all environmental health and safety laws and to assure equal protection of the public health. The Act mandated data collection to identify counties in the United States where populations are exposed to disproportionately greater discharges of toxic substances. No action was taken on this proposal, but it may be reintroduced in the 103rd Congress. Concerns about limited involvement of communities in decisions to issue permits to solid waste treatment and disposal facilities were addressed in H.R. 3865 and S. 976, bills to reauthorize and amend the Solid Waste Disposal Act, but neither bill was enacted. Either measure would have increased opportunities for citizens to influence permitting decisions. The House bill also required permit decisions to consider demographic characteristics of the host community and the cumulative effect on the host community of existing and proposed facilities and sites.

Congress did act to control lead hazards. It considered two comprehensive lead bills, S. 391 and H.R. 5730. These directed EPA to monitor new and existing uses of lead and to identify and control major sources of exposure. Lead-based paint in existing housing was targeted by both bills, as well as by Title X of H.R. 5334, the Housing and Community Development Act of 1992. Lead in drinking water was addressed in S. 1445 and H.R. 5730. As the 102d Congress drew to a close, certain provisions of H.R. 5730, relating to certification and training of contractors, were incorporated into Title X of H.R. 5334 (H.Rept. 102-1017,) which was then cleared for the President and signed into law Oct. 28, 1992. The enacted legislation (P.L. 102-550) redirects Federal lead-based paint policy to prevent lead poisoning by targeting Federal efforts to identify and reduce actual, as opposed to potential, hazards and permitting use of interim measures to reduce immediate and severe risks to children. It authorizes $375,000,000 to be appropriated over 2 years for grants to assess and control lead-based paint hazards in private housing occupied by low-income families with young children. Owners of residential real estate must notify prospective buyers and tenants of any known lead hazards.

Recent studies indicate that black Americans and other racial and ethnic minorities may be exposed to more pollution and bear greater health risks due to the poor quality of their environment than whites. Although the level of exposure to toxic substances also is related to income level, income alone does not seem to account for the uneven distribution of environmental hazards.

To assess the extent and severity of environmental inequities, the Environmental Protection Agency organized the Environmental Equity Workgroup in 1990. In its final report, released July 22, 1992, the Workgroup concluded, "There are clear differences between racial groups in terms of disease and death rates. There are also limited data to explain the environmental contribution to these differences ... Racial minority and low-income populations experience higher than average exposures to selected air pollutants, hazardous waste facilities, contaminated fish and agricultural pesticides in the workplace ... A significantly higher percentage of black children compared to white children have unacceptably high blood-lead levels." EPA established an Environmental Equity Office within the Office of Administration and Resources Management to oversee and coordinate implementation of the Workgroup's recommendations. The new EPA Administrator, Carol Browner, has made environmental justice one of her top four priorities for EPA.

During the 102nd Congress, legislation (P.L. 102-550) was enacted to redirect and expedite Federal lead-based paint poisoning prevention efforts to better address the needs of low-income communities.

Several bills promoting environmental justice have been introduced in the 103rd Congress. The Environmental Justice Act (H.R. 2105) requires EPA to identify the 100 geographic areas of the United States with the greatest quantity of toxic chemicals based on weight and toxicity. Health effects of these toxic chemicals on people residing in the 100 locations are to be assessed, and if significant health effects are found, the President is required to propose legislative remedies. In addition, the legislation proposes a moratorium on the siting and issuance of permits for new toxic chemical facilities and compliance inspections by EPA of existing toxic chemical facilities within communities with health effects.

Other legislative proposals encourage environmental testing or clean up of hazardous wastes to permit economic redevelopment of urban areas (H.R. 1005, S. 100, S. 299, S. 522, and S. 773); allow citizens to petition to prevent certain hazardous and solid waste management facilities from being constructed in "environmentally disadvantaged communities" (H.R. 1924); and require the Agency for Toxic Substances and Disease Registry to collect data on "the race, age, gender, ethnic origin, income level, and educational level of persons living in communities adjacent to toxic substance contamination" (H.R. 1925). A recently passed Senate bill, S. 171, requires EPA to maintain an Office of Environmental Justice. A discussion draft of a House bill to elevate EPA to department status also requires an Office of Environmental Justice within EPA. In addition, the House draft establishes an advisory committee, a research program, and several grant programs, and requires enforcement of the Civil Rights Act of 1964 to ensure that programs financed by EPA do not result in a pattern of exposure to environmental hazards that is discriminatory on the basis of race, color, or national origin.

Foreign Affairs

The Caribbean

The end of the Cold War has shifted U.S. interests in the Caribbean from an emphasis on security concerns to a new focus on economic and other issues. Some believe an important challenge for policymakers is to maintain an active U.S. interest in the region despite the cessation of Cold War tensions and the greater economic importance of the larger Latin American economies. U.S. policy toward the region has several components, including strengthening democracy and advancing human rights; supporting economic growth and development; and curbing illegal immigration and the flow of illicit drugs into the United States.

In the area of democracy and human rights, congressional concerns center on the countries of Cuba, Haiti, and Guyana. Congress condemned human rights violations in Cuba in 1991, and in 1992 Congress approved legislation tightening existing trade restrictions on Cuba in order to hasten change in the hemisphere's only Communist country. Congress also went on record condemning the September 1991 coup in Haiti which overthrew that nation's first democratically elected president, and there was concern expressed in Congress about the future direction of U.S. policy in supporting a return to democratic rule (see section below on **Haiti**). In Guyana, congressional concerns were satisfied when free and fair elections were held on Oct. 5, 1992, ending almost 30 years of rule by one party.

In the area of economic growth and development, the Caribbean is home to the hemisphere's poorest as well as some of its richest nations. To promote growth and development, the United States employs three policy tools: economic and food assistance; trade and investment promotion; and debt-reduction. In recent years,

Members of Congress have expressed concern about declining levels of assistance to the Caribbean. With regard to trade and investment promotion, some in Congress expressed concern about how the Caribbean will fare within the framework of a North American Free Trade Area. With regard to debt reduction, in 1990 Congress provided authority to reduce U.S. food assistance debt owed by Latin American and Caribbean nations, and legislation was approved in 1991 giving the Administration authority to forgive additional types of debt owed to the U.S. Government. Reduction of U.S. official debt is especially significant for several Caribbean nations that owe a large portion of their external debt to the U.S. Government, although some argue that such debt forgiveness transfers the debt from foreigners to U.S. taxpayers. In 1991, the United States forgave $430 million of U.S. official debt owed by three Caribbean nations: Guyana, Haiti, and Jamaica.

In the war against drugs, the United States provides substantial assistance to the region through a variety of U.S. agencies, including interdiction and law enforcement support. Most Caribbean nations cooperate with the United States in anti-narcotics efforts, but U.S. officials have expressed concern about the slow pace of Caribbean nations in adopting effective measures against drug money laundering.

Haiti

On Sept. 30, 1991, Jean-Bertrand Aristide, Haiti's first democratically elected president, was overthrown in a military coup after serving only 8 months of a 5-year term. The *de facto* government and the military refused to accept a February 1992 accord, brokered by the Organization of American States (OAS), that would have paved the way for Aristide's return. Instead, a new prime minister, Marc Bazin, was sworn in on June 19, 1992, without consulting Aristide. Efforts are now focussed on OAS-sponsored talks between representatives of Aristide and the *de facto* regime. The first round of talks, which ended Sept. 4, 1992, resulted in a tentative agreement for sending 18 OAS observers to Haiti. The United States and the OAS have called for Aristide's reinstatement, which is apparently desired by the mostly poor populace who elected him overwhelmingly but is resisted by several influential sectors of Haitian society. The United States cut off aid to the current Haitian regime (although humanitarian aid continued through private voluntary organizations) and, in compliance with an OAS embargo, banned most U.S. trade with that nation.

Congress's main foreign policy concern is how to restore democracy to Haiti. If the embargo does not force the *de facto* government to allow Aristide's return, Congress may have to decide whether to support continuing the embargo, which is contributing to the increased suffering of Haiti's poor, or to consider other options, including a multilateral civilian observer group or military intervention. If Aristide's return is arranged, the international community will face issues such as Aristide's personal security and his ability to govern effectively and democratically. Some observers question the wisdom of insisting on Aristide's return, due in part to what many see as Aristide's contributions to tensions. Whether Aristide is excluded or returned, a violent popular backlash is possible.

The dramatic increase of Haitians setting sail for the United States following the coup has raised legal and moral questions about current immigration policies toward Haitian migrants, as well as prompted congressional action. Since the military ousted President Aristide, about 40,000 Haitians have been interdicted by the Coast Guard, and many were detained at the U.S. naval base in Guantanamo Bay, Cuba. After declining in February and March, interdictions rose in April and May. Prior to May 24, those Haitians successfully pre-screened were allowed to apply for asylum in the United States. Haitians pre-screened with plausible asylum claims have fluctuated, reaching a high of almost 40% in March, falling under 10% in April, and rising again to almost 40% in mid-May. The State Department maintains that there is no evidence that any of the repatriated Haitians have been harmed.

On May 24, 1992, President Bush issued an executive order that instructed the Coast Guard to intercept and immediately return all Haitians in boats on the high seas without interviewing them to determine whether they are at risk of persecution if returned. Instead, Haitians may apply for refugee status at the Embassy in Port-au-Prince. Haitian refugee advocates claimed that the repatriation violated the principle of nonrefoulement (i.e., that an alien will not be returned to a country where that person's life or freedom would be threatened). The Administration pointed out that the Haitians interdicted have not crossed into the territorial limits of the United States and, thus, are not entitled to the protections of the U.S. Constitution or the Immigration and Nationality Act. A legal challenge to Bush's latest executive order is before the U.S. Supreme Court.

The crux of the immigration issue is twofold: whether Haitian migrants are viewed as fleeing persecution or poverty; and, whether the safety of Haitian boat people can be ensured when they are forced to return to Haiti. In February, the House passed H.R. 3844 that would, among other things, halt repatriations for 180 days and establish refugee processing for Haitians. The House and Senate also considered legislation which would have affirmed that nonrefoulement applies to asylum seekers outside of U.S. territory.

Haiti's first democratically elected president was overthrown in September 1991, propelling Haiti into its worst crisis since the collapse of the 29-year Duvalier family dictatorship in 1986. President Jean-Bertrand Aristide, elected with two-thirds of the vote, was ousted in a military coup after serving only 8 months of a 5-year term. For over a year and a half the de facto regime has resisted international pressure to return Aristide to office, including an Organization of American States (OAS) embargo and the suspension of most foreign aid. The de facto government installed by the military refused to accept an OAS-brokered accord in February 1992 that would have paved the way for Aristide's return. Instead, in June a new prime minister, Marc Bazin, was sworn in, without consulting Aristide.

Several other OAS diplomatic initiatives in 1992 were unsuccessful, but hopes for a political resolution were revived when the United Nations (UN) became involved late in the year. U.N. Special Envoy Dante Caputo began holding meetings in Haiti in December. On Feb. 9, 1993, the Haitian regime reversed its position and agreed to accept an OAS/U.N. civilian observer mission to oversee the restoration of order and monitor human rights conditions. By the end of March about 140 observers were in Haiti, and negotiations were continuing for a return to democratic rule. Among the issues to be resolved are the date of Aristide's return; the structure of an interim government; the fate of the coup leaders; and the personal safety of persons on both sides.

In March 1993, President Clinton named retired Ambassador Lawrence Pezzullo as special adviser on Haiti and met with Aristide. Clinton warned that opposition to Aristide's return would be met with stronger U.S. measures. He also committed the United States to its "fair portion" of a 5-year, $1 billion plan he proposed to rebuild Haiti's economy and said an aide would examine conditions at Guantanamo Bay Naval Base, where over 200 Haitians who fled Haiti remain detained. Some observers praise Clinton's actions as unequivocal support for the restoration of democracy. Others criticize him for not being forceful enough, or for the reversal of his stand on Haitian migrants.

South Africa

The Comprehensive Antiapartheid Act of 1986 (P.L. 99-440) imposed sanctions against South Africa because of its apartheid policies. Congressional debate on sanctions in recent years has centered on whether or not sanctions should be lifted. In 1991, some in Congress wanted the sanctions to remain until black South African leaders indicated that they should be lifted. African National Congress (ANC) leader Nelson Mandela asked U.N. members in December 1991 to wait until an interim government was established before lifting financial sanctions. The ANC argues that sanctions are necessary to keep pressure on Pretoria so that it will agree to an interim government and a new nonracial constitution. Others in Congress believed that the government of President F.W. De Klerk should be rewarded for its reforms and its commitment to negotiations. The Administration advocated lifting sanctions as soon as all the conditions in the 1986 Act were met. These conditions included releasing Nelson Mandela and other political prisoners, ending the banning of certain organizations, repealing basic apartheid laws, and committing to negotiating a new nonracial and democratic constitution.

On July 10, 1991, President Bush lifted the sanctions in the 1986 Act. He justified his action by saying the De Klerk government's reforms and commitment to negotiations were irreversible and that lifting sanctions would encourage the economic growth needed to meet the rising expectations of black South Africans. Despite the President's action, several sanctions under other legislation remained and other sanctions imposed by State and local governments continued. The remaining sanctions have deterred many U.S. businesses from resuming relations with South Africa. Formal negotiations began between black leaders and the De Klerk government in December 1991. Negotiations broke down in June 1992, but in September the government and the ANC agreed to resume formal negotiations. Although both sides agree there is no alternative to negotiations, increasing violence is making this difficult. Nevertheless, a provisional date of late November was set for further bilateral talks between the government and the ANC on resumption of multiparty negotiations.

To aid South Africans disadvantaged by apartheid, the United States provided $38.4 million in FY1991; to promote democracy in South Africa, an additional $10 million was obligated. There was debate in 1991 over whether the ANC should receive part of the $10 million. In spite of this debate, by July 1992 the Agency for International Development had plans to distribute large portions of these funds to both the ANC and to the Inkatha Freedom Party. For FY1992 an estimated $80 million was obligated, and another $80 million was requested by the Administration for FY1993.

The United States imposed sanctions against South Africa in 1986 because of its apartheid policies. These sanctions, which were part of the Comprehensive Antiapartheid Act of 1986 (P.L. 99-440), were lifted by the Bush Administration in July 1991. Some in Congress wanted the sanctions to remain until black South African leaders agreed to their lifting. The African National Congress (ANC) has favored keeping sanctions in place until an interim government is established, but in 1993 ANC President Nelson Mandela reportedly said that he may call for the lifting of sanctions once a date is set for the election of a constituent assembly that will draft a new constitution for a non-racial democratic political system. The tentative change of policy has been prompted by the ANC's concern for massive unemployment in South Africa. In addition to the 1986 sanctions, the United States has kept in place several other sanctions imposed by earlier legislation and a 1991 ban on trade with South African entities involved in missile technology. Numerous State and local sanctions against South Africa also remain. The new Administration must decide at what point these remaining sanctions should be lifted, and Congress may want to have some input into that decision.

Formal negotiations for a nonracial and democratic government began in December 1991, but by June 1992 the talks had stalled because of disagreements over issues and rampant violence in the country. Nevertheless, in September the government and the ANC agreed to resume negotiations. Bilateral discussions between the government and various political parties were held throughout the remainder of 1992 and early in the new year. On April 1, multilateral negotiations were held, but they were almost derailed by the assassination of Chris Hani, the head of the South African Communist Party and a prominent leader of the ANC, and the ensuing violent demonstrations. Nonetheless, the negotiating parties resolved to continue the talks. By June 3, they had tentatively agreed on a date (Apr. 27, 1994) for the first non-racial election of a constituent assembly.

A transitional or interim government is expected to be established several months before the elections. Once the transitional government becomes a reality, both Congress and the Clinton Administration may want to reconsider the amount of aid the United States provides and what areas of aid might be emphasized. In FY1992, an estimated $80 million was obligated for disadvantaged South Africans, and another $80 million was requested by the Administration for FY1993. An additional $10 million was appropriated in May 1990 to promote democracy in South Africa. These funds, however, were not distributed until 1992, and the largest portions were provided to the ANC and the Inkatha Freedom Party.

Black Americans:
Issues and Concerns

ISBN 1-56072-173-1

FEDERAL RESEARCH AND DEVELOPMENT FUNDING AT HISTORICALLY BLACK COLLEGES AND UNIVERSITIES*

C.M. Matthews

SUMMARY

Many observers believe that historically black colleges and universities (HBCUs) have not shared equitably in the distribution of Federal research and development (R&D) obligations to colleges and universities. Because of lack of resources and inadequate infrastructure, many of these institutions are unable to engage in cutting edge scientific research at the level of many non-HBCUs. Federal R&D funding to HBCUs has increased in the past 10 years in absolute terms, however it remains approximately 1 percent of the total awarded to all institutions. By way of comparison, research performing HBCUs are 12.7 percent of all U.S. institutions receiving Federal research funding. A 1992 report of the National Science Foundation, *Federal Support to Universities, Colleges, and Nonprofit Institutions: Fiscal Year 1990*, indicated that for fiscal year 1990, HBCUs received approximately $101 million for R&D (of $9,031 million awarded to all institutions), an increase of $8.9 million (9.7 percent) over the fiscal year 1989 level of $92.1 million (of $8,522.6 million awarded to all institutions).

While estimates vary on the level of research facilities expenditures at all institutions of higher education ($7 billion to $12 billion), the crisis of deteriorating physical plant and backlog of maintenance at HBCUs is very severe. Approximately 70 percent of the HBCUs were established prior to 1900. Some even have aging facilities with electrical systems that are inadequate for the loads that complex computer systems and other state-of-the-art equipment (if available) would require.

* Excerpted from CIS Report 93-538.

In a National Science Foundation (NSF) survey of 70 research-performing HBCUs, the institutions reported beginning approximately $37.6 million in research facility construction projects in school year 1990-91. These same institutions also reported that there was no anticipation of increasing construction of research facilities for school year 1992-93. Projections were that construction for school year 1992-93 would not exceed $13 million, approximately 34.6 percent of the previous time period.

INTRODUCTION

The historically black colleges and universities (HBCUs), which have traditionally educated a significant number of the Nation's blacks, have faced and continue to face substantial challenges in attempting to enhance their academic and research capabilities and developing programs to compete with other institutions of higher education. These black institutions have a plethora of problems--inadequate support for student aid, deteriorating laboratories, lack of access to resources required for scientific research, obsolete equipment, low salary structures, and limited funds for faculty development and new academic programs for students. While these problems exist in other institutions, they appear to be substantially more serious in HBCUs.

The changing external environment (increasing public demand for institutional accountability and effectiveness) and new competitive conditions in higher education (decline in Federal support coupled with spiraling costs of research) have made it increasingly harder for HBCUs to develop and expand their research programs.[1] Because of the level of financial resources (Federal, State, and private) these institutions generally have received, many are unable to engage in cutting edge scientific research at the level of many non-HBCUs. Many HBCUs face difficulty competing for scarce research dollars with other research-performing universities.

Amid criticism by officials and representatives of HBCUs concerning the disparity in their receipt of Federal research and development (R&D) support, several executive orders were issued, designed to strengthen and increase the

---

[1] For expanded discussion of the changing climate in academia, see for example, U.S. Library of Congress. Congressional Research Service. American Science at a Critical Crossroads. CRS Issue Brief IB92016, by Genevieve J. Knezo. Washington, Apr. 4, 1973. 15 p. (continually updated); Lepkowski, Wil. University Research: Heyday of Science Seen As Over. Chemical and Engineering News, v. 69, Dec. 9, 1991. p. 4; Ostling, Richard N. Big Chill on Campus. Time, Feb. 3, 1992. p. 61-63; Fateful Choices: The Future of the U.S. Academic Research Enterprise. A Discussion Paper. Government-University-Industry Research Roundtable. Washington, 1992. 58 p.

participation of the HBCUs in federally sponsored programs.[2] In addition to increasing the participation of HBCUs in research and improving the administrative infrastructure of the institutions, the executive orders were also designed to ". . . eliminate barriers which may have unfairly resulted in reduced participation in, and reduced benefits from, federally-sponsored programs."[3]

In 1990, the Bush Administration proposed to categorize and classify HBCUs based on their missions and programs. The premise was that it would allow Federal agencies to select the "appropriate group" for developing linkages, rather than having them work with the various programs in all the institutions. Considerable criticism voiced by presidents and department chairs of HBCUs contributed to the withdrawal of the proposal. Opposition was based on the concern that only a small group of the institutions would receive funding--those that were already considered to be the research "elite." As a consequence, there were fears the remainder might be abandoned.[4]

Demographic data show a future with proportionately fewer young people and an increasingly larger portion of the workforce comprised of minorities and the economically disadvantaged. The Bureau of the Census predicts that by the year 2020, blacks and Hispanics will constitute more than 35 percent of the total population of the United States. These groups, on which the economy must increasingly rely, have traditionally been underrepresented in the sciences compared to their fraction of the total population. Although HBCUs have played an important role in providing the undergraduate preparation for many of those black students entering highly specialized science and engineering disciplines, their efforts at attracting, retaining, preparing, and graduating students in the sciences may need to be expanded in order to respond to demographic realities. Many observers believe the problem of underrepresented minorities in the sciences could compromise the United States' ability to develop and advance its traditional industrial base and to compete in international marketplaces.

HISTORICAL BACKGROUND

Historically black colleges and universities are defined as those institutions ". . . established prior to 1964, whose principal mission was the education of

---

[2] The various executive orders include Executive Order 12232, Aug. 1980; Executive Order 12320, Sept. 1981; and Executive Order 12677, Apr. 1989.

[3] United States Code. Congressional and Administrative News, 97th Cong. 1st Session, West Publishing Co., St. Paul, NM, 1981. p. 77.

[4] Mercer, Joye. White House Scraps Classification Plan for Black Institutions. Black Issues in Higher Education, v. 8, May 23, 1991. p. 7.

black Americans."[5] While three HBCUs were established prior to the Civil War, the majority of these institutions were established after the War, several with the public support of land grants through the Freedman's Bureau.[6] The First Morrill Act, (National Land-Grant Colleges Act of 1862), provided public lands to various States for the purpose of constructing educational institutions.[7] Funds appropriated under this act were distributed to the states ". . . [W]ith the intention that they would foster equal educational opportunities for all students, especially newly freed blacks."[8] However, the land-grant higher education system resulting from the First Morrill Act failed to provide equal educational opportunities. As a result, black students were excluded from enrolling in traditionally white institutions.

> Funds from the Morrill Act began to flow systemically to schools offering only all-white education. Congress attempted by various legislation to force racial equality, including equality of educational opportunity. However, the U.S. Supreme Court initiated a series of interpretations of the post-Civil War constitutional amendments which ultimately defeated these various legislative efforts. Culminating with its landmark 1882 decision finding the first Civil Rights Act [1866] unconstitutional, the Supreme Court held that the 14th amendment only protected against direct discriminatory action by a State government.[9]

A Second Morrill Act was passed in 1890, which included language mandating States with dual systems of higher education to provide land-grant institutions for both systems. As a result 19 institutions were established as black land-grant institutions, enrolling those black students who had been excluded under the 1862 legislation. (For a listing of the 1890 land-grant institutions, see table A in the appendix.) While there was the creation of two land-grant systems--one established under the 1862 Land-Grant Act (First Morrill Act) and the other under the 1890 Land-Grant Act (Second Morrill Act)--the level of support for the 1890 institutions (both Federal and State) never

---

[5] U.S. Dept. of Education. Historically Black Colleges and Universities, 1976-90. Edited by Hoffman, Charlene M., Thomas D. Snyder, and Bill Sonnenberg. Washington, U.S. Govt. Print. Off., 1992. p. 1.

[6] The Freedman's Bureau operated from 1865-1873 to provide assistance for newly freed slaves. Ibid., p. 2.

[7] The establishment of a public land-grant system is considered to be one of the most significant developments in U.S. higher education. Prior to the First Morrill Act, higher education opportunities were limited to the very elite.

[8] U.S. Dept. of Education. Historically Black Colleges and Universities, 1976-90, op. cit., p. 2.

[9] Ibid.

approximated the level received by the 1862 land-grant institutions.[10] In particular, during the expansion of program offerings and disciplines at the 1890 institutions, the disparity in funding for research infrastructure between them and the earlier established institutions severely limited their efforts to support basic and applied research.[11] In written testimony before the House Committee on Agriculture in support of legislation providing assistance to 1890 institutions, Honorable Harold E. Ford noted that:

> ... [T]he 1890 institutions were never adequately funded the way they should have been by the various states. With assistance from the various states and Federal Government, the 1862 institutions were permitted to thrive and expand, while the 1890 institutions received meager funding from both their respective state and Federal Government.
>
> Furthermore, the 1890 institutions were not eligible to participate in the facilities programs provided in the late 1960s and early 1970s by the Federal Government. Under the Research Facilities Act of 1963, only the 1862 land-grant institutions were permitted to participate in this program. Not until 1967 did the Federal Government start to provide research funds to the 1890 programs. These funds were for research projects, and not for constructing research facilities.[12]

CLASSIFICATION OF HBCUs

The diversity of HBCUs parallels that of other institutions of higher education. HBCUs (primarily located in the South) are composed of public and private; single-sex and coed; predominantly black and predominantly white; 2-year and 4-year institutions, research universities, liberal arts colleges, and

---

[10] For expanded discussion of land-grant institutions, see for example, McDowell, George R. Land-Grant Colleges of Agriculture: Renegotiating or Abandoning A Social Contract. Choices, v. 22, Second Quarter 1988. p. 18-21; and Schuh, G. Edward. Revitalizing Land-Grant Universities. Choices, Second Quarter 1986. p. 6-10.

[11] Most HBCUs began as "normal" schools--with the fundamental mission to train teachers. Beginning in the late 1960s and early 1970s, there was a shift in that focus to other professions. However, HBCUs continue to graduate and award a large number of degrees in education.

[12] In 1967, the Federal Government provided **$285,000** to be divided among 16 - 1890 land-grant institutions (approximately $17,812.50 per institution). U.S. Congress. House. Committee on Agriculture. Subcommittee on Dept. Operations, Research, and Foreign Agriculture. Hearing on H.R. 1309, 1890 Land-Grant Colleges Facilities. 97th Cong., 1st Session, June 4, 1981. Washington, U.S. Govt. Print. Off., 1981. p. 13-15.

professional schools.[13] The U.S Department of Education reports that, currently, there are 105 HBCUs--40 public 4-year colleges, 11 public 2-year colleges, 46 private 4-year colleges, 5 private 2-year colleges, and 3 private professional schools.[14] Of the 105 HBCUs listed by the Department of Education, 70 are classified by the National Science Foundation (NSF) as research-performing institutions.[15] For a listing of all HBCUs with relevant information, see table B in the appendix.

While HBCUs represent approximately 3 percent of all institutions of higher education, they enroll approximately 17 percent of black students attending post-secondary institutions.[16] In addition, some of the most successful programs designed to attract underrepresented minorities into the sciences and research careers have been initiated at HBCUs.[17] (Approximately 47 percent of the undergraduate degrees awarded to blacks from Xavier

---

[13] Fall 1990 enrollment data reveal that five HBCUs have predominantly white student populations--Bluefield State College (91.9 percent), West Virginia State College (86.6 percent), J. F. Drake Technical College (62.9 percent), Lincoln University, Missouri (73.3 percent), and Kentucky State University (53.1 percent). Historically Black Colleges and Universities, 1976-90, op. cit., p. 32-33.

[14] Data of the Department of Education reveal that there are 2,157 4-year institutions, and 1,444 2-year institutions. Disaggregated data reveal that HBCUs are approximately 4 percent of all 4-year institutions and approximately 1 percent of all 2-year institutions. For expanded discussion of HBCUs, see for example, U.S. Library of Congress. Congressional Research Service. Historically Black Colleges and Universities and African-American Participation in Higher Education. CRS Report 89-588 RCO, by William W. Ellis and James B. Stedman. Washington, 1989. 74 p.

[15] U.S. National Science Foundation. Scientific and Engineering Research Facilities at Universities and Colleges: 1992. NSF 92-325, Sept. 1992. p. 6-1.

[16] HBCUs have become quite diverse. For example, the major predominantly white universities have approximately 6% black student population while the HBCUs have about 11% white student population.

[17] The underrepresented minorities include blacks, Hispanics, Native Americans, and women. Asian Americans are excluded because they are not statistically underrepresented in science, mathematics, and engineering. See for example, U.S. Library of Congress. Congressional Research Service. Underrepresented Minorities and Women in Science, Mathematics, and Engineering: Problems and Issues for the 1990s. CRS Report 91-26 SPR, by Christine M. Matthews. Washington, 1992. 76 p.; and Culotta, Elizabeth. Black Colleges Cultivate Scientists. Science, v. 258, Nov. 13, 1992. p. 1216-1218. Engineering is a discipline that has witnessed an increased participation of blacks. What is unique about this discipline is that many of the degrees are awarded from HBCUs that do not have their own engineering schools, but do have cooperative programs based at neighboring major research universities.

University are in science and mathematics. The institution has received national recognition for its model science program.) Data from the National Research Council indicate that a significant number of students graduating from bachelor and masters programs at HBCUs further their studies in doctoral programs at predominantly white universities. For years 1985-1991, the HBCUs provided the undergraduate education for approximately 67 percent of blacks earning doctorate degree in computer sciences, 42 percent in biological sciences, 35 percent in agricultural sciences, 29 percent in physical sciences, and 23 percent in mathematics.[18] Reginald Wilson, senior scholar of the American Council on Education's Office of Minority Concerns, stated that this preparation of minority scientists is: ". . . [A] tribute to the black colleges' unique capacity to instill confidence in students, and to their special dedication to nurturing talent through methods like mentoring."[19]

FEDERAL RESEARCH AND DEVELOPMENT SUPPORT TO HBCUs

An important issue in the academic community, and in science policy in general, is the distribution of Federal research and development (R&D) funds to colleges and universities. A major criticism of Federal R&D funding patterns is that there is concentration in certain colleges and universities, contributing to the maintenance of existing scientific capabilities. (The elite institutions ("haves") continue in their status, and the less-prestigious scientific institutions ("havenots") continue to struggle.) Equity considerations involved in R&D funding include those of geographic distribution on a per capita basis, merit review (especially peer review) of research proposals, and selection of colleges and universities to receive funds, especially HBCUs.[20] For the purposes of this report, the discussion will focus on the last consideration, the distribution of Federal R&D funding to colleges and universities, including HBCUs. While various measures of equity can be calculated--e. g., based on the number of institutions, student enrollments, science and engineering students, graduate students--the following analysis will examine Federal obligations for R&D to HBCUs as a percentage of all research performing institutions.

---

[18] U.S. National Science Foundation. HBCUs and the Baccalaureate Origins of Recent Doctorate Recipients. Presented at the 18th National Conference on Blacks in Higher Education, by Susan Hill and Eliza Hizell. Washington, Apr. 3, 1993. p. 1.

[19] Wycliff, Don. Blacks Advance Slow in Science Career. New York Times, June 8, 1990. p. A14.

[20] For expanded discussion of distribution of Federal R&D to colleges and universities, see for example, U.S. Library of Congress. Congressional Research Service. Equity, Excellence, and the Distribution of Federal Research and Development Funds. CRS Report 88-422 SPR, by William C. Boesman and Christine Matthews Rose. Washington, 1988. 88 p.

The NSF reports that approximately 550 U.S. academic institutions conduct research and development (R&D), of which 70 are classified as research-performing HBCUs.[21] Trend data reveal that these research-performing HBCUs have not shared proportionately in the distribution of Federal R&D obligations to colleges and universities.[22] Although funding to HBCUs has increased in the past 10 years in absolute terms, it remains only a small fraction of the total awarded to all U.S. colleges and universities. A 1992 report of the NSF, *Federal Support to Universities, Colleges, and Nonprofit Institutions: Fiscal Year 1990,* indicated that for fiscal year 1990, HBCUS received approximately $101 million for R&D, an increase of $8.9 million (9.7 percent) over the fiscal year 1989 level of $92.1 million.[23] Data from 1980-1990 reveal that while research performing HBCUs are approximately 12.7 percent of all U.S. institutions conducting R&D, they receive approximately 1 percent of all Federal academic R&D support. Table 1 below provides the levels of R&D support for fiscal years 1980 through 1990.

---

[21] See *supra* note 15.

[22] See for example, Mercer, Joye. Black-College Advisory Board Faults Federal Research Spending. The Chronicle of Higher Education, v. 39, Jan. 13, 1993. p. A26.

The data on Federal support to academic R&D result from a compilation of 15 agencies. Research and development includes all research activities, both basic and applied, and all development activities that are supported at colleges and universities. Obligations reported do not include funds to federally-funded research and development centers (FFRDCs).

[23] The institutions compiling this population are those receiving current year obligations. Caution should be exercised in reviewing the data. Because of the relatively small number of HBCUs, data from a few institutions can skew the quantitative findings and have a substantial effect on the resulting analysis. U.S. National Science Foundation. Federal Support to Universities, Colleges, and Nonprofit Institutions: Fiscal Year 1990. Detailed Statistical Tables. NSF 92-324. Washington, 1992. p. 58-59.

TABLE 1.
Federal Obligations for Research and Development to Research-Performing Historically Black Colleges and Universities as a Percentage of Total Academic Research and Development Support, Fiscal Years 1980-1990[a]
(in millions)

	R&D to All Research Institutions	R&D to HBCUs	HBCUs as % of Total
1980	$4,160.5	$36.5	1.0
1981	4,410.9	39.8	1.0
1982	4,554.5	40.5	1.0
1983	5,024.3	49.1	1.0
1984	5,448.8	50.3	1.0
1985	6,246.2	56.6	1.0
1986	6,456.7	57.0	1.0
1987	7,241.0	62.6	1.0
1988	7,719.2	62.8	1.0
1989	8,522.6	92.1	1.1
1990	9,031.0	101.0	1.1

[a] Federal Support to Universities, Colleges, and Nonprofit Institutions: Fiscal Year 1990, op. cit., p. 13, 58; and U.S. National Science Foundation. Federal Support to Universities, Colleges, and Selected Nonprofit Institutions: Fiscal Year 1986. NSF 87-318. p. 74.

An analysis of Federal R&D support to HBCUs shows that funding is concentrated at selected institutions. (Funding for non-HBCUs also is concentrated at selected institutions).[24] In fiscal year 1990, the top ten institutions (in terms of receipt of Federal R&D) accounted for approximately 62.9 percent of total Federal R&D support, and the top 20 institutions accounted for approximately 84.9 percent of total R&D support. (In fiscal year 1980, the top 10 HBCUs received 56.8 percent of funding to these institutions, and the top 20 institutions received 85.4 percent of funding). In addition,

[24] See for example, U.S. Library of Congress. Congressional Research Service. Equity, Excellence, and the Distribution of Federal Research and Development Funds. CRS Report 88-422 SPR, by William C. Boesman and Christine Matthews Rose. Washington, 1988. 88 p.

Howard University, which has consistently ranked number one in terms of Federal R&D support among HBCUs, commanded 15.4 percent of total Federal R&D funding to HBCUs. (In fiscal year 1980, Howard University received 19.7 percent of all Federal R&D support to HBCUs).[25]

Table 2 below provides a listing of the top 20 HBCUs and their level of funding. The rankings (by amounts received in fiscal year 1990) reveal that there has been only relative change in the concentration of Federal R&D support among the top 20 HBCUs since 1980. Five of the top 10 HBCUs in fiscal year 1990 also were ranked in the top 10 for fiscal year 1980 (four in different ordinal positions). More noticeable is that 15 of the top 20 institutions in fiscal year 1990, also were among the top 20 institutions in fiscal year 1980 (in different ordinal positions). However, a few institutions have received increased support so as to change their ranking. In fiscal year 1990, Clark Atlanta University ranked second in R&D support, in fiscal year 1980, it ranked twentieth.[26] Hampton University which ranked third in fiscal year 1990, was ranked twenty-second in fiscal year 1980. Florida A&M University, ranked eighth in fiscal year 1990, was ranked seventeenth in fiscal year 1980. And the Morehouse School of Medicine, which was not eligible for funding in 1980 (had not received accreditation), ranked sixth in fiscal year 1990.[27]

---

[25] Howard University, while primarily publicly funded since 1928, continues to maintain the status of a private institution.

[26] Note: In 1980, Clark College and Atlanta University were two separate institutions. Total funding (merged data) for the two institutions was $0.8 million. The fiscal year 1980 ranking was based on this total. These two institutions merged in 1989 and became Clark Atlanta University.

[27] Morehouse School of Medicine began in 1975 as a medical program within Morehouse College. In April 1985, the school was granted full accreditation to award an MD degree.

TABLE 2.
Federal Obligations for Research and Development to the Top 20 HBCUs in Descending Order of Total Amount Received: Fiscal Year 1980 and 1990[a]
(dollars in millions)

	Fiscal Year 1980	Fiscal Year 1990
Institutions (ranked by amount received in fiscal year 1990)		
1. Howard University	7.2	15.5 (1)[b]
2. Clark Atlanta University	0.8	7.9 (20)
3. Meharry Medical College	1.2	6.6 (13)
4. North Carolina A&T State University	2.2	6.1 (3)
5. Hampton University	0.6	5.1 (22)
6. Morehouse School of Medicine	--[c]	4.9 ( )
7. Alabama A&M University	1.8	4.7 (4)
8. Florida A&M University	0.9	4.5 (17)
9. Tuskegee University	2.6	4.2 (2)
10. Tennessee State University	1.4	4.0 (8)
11. Prairie View A&M University	1.7	3.3 (5)
12. Jackson State University	0.5	3.1 (23)
13. Kentucky State University	1.5	2.4 (6)
14. Virginia State University	1.2	2.2 (10)
15. Southern University & A&M College	1.3	2.1 (9)
16. Fort Valley State College	1.4	2.0 (7)
17. Lincoln University (MO)	1.2	1.9 (12)
18. University of Maryland Eastern Shore	0.9	1.9 (16)
19. Texas Southern University	0.3	1.8 (25)
20. Xavier University of LA	1.0	1.5 (30)

[a] U.S. National Science Foundation. Federal Support to Universities, Colleges, and Selected Nonprofit Institutions: Fiscal Year 1985. Detailed Statistical Tables. Washington, 1985. p. 61; and Federal Support to Universities, Colleges, and Nonprofit Institutions: Fiscal Year 1990, op. cit., p. 58.

[b] Numbers in ( ) are rankings for fiscal year 1980.

[c] See *supra* note 26.

RESEARCH FACILITIES AT HBCUs

A 1989 publication, *The Decaying American Campus: A Ticking Time Bomb,* noted that facility construction/modernization/maintenance probably represents the largest capital investment for institutions of higher education. The quality of an institutions' facilities is vital to the quality of education offered.[28] While estimates vary on the level of deferred research facilities expenditures at all institutions of higher education ($7 billion to $12 billion), the crisis of deteriorating physical plant and backlog of maintenance at HBCUs is even more severe.[29] Approximately 70 percent of the HBCUs were established prior to 1900 (60 percent date from before 1890). Some have aging facilities with electrical systems that are inadequate for the loads that complex computer systems and other state-of-the-art equipment (if available) would require.[30]

In a NSF 1992 survey of 70 research-performing HBCUs, the institutions reported beginning approximately $37.6 million in research facility construction projects in school year 1990-91.[31] These same institutions also reported that there was no anticipation of increasing construction of research facilities for school year 1992-93. The converse existed. Projections were that construction for school year 1992-93 would not exceed $13 million, approximately 34.6 percent of the previous time period.

Aggregate data were collected from a reduced sample of 29 institutions (out of the population of 70) in order to compare research facility construction with similar surveys conducted in 1988 and 1990. This separate analysis of 29 HBCUs revealed that research facility construction had witnessed a significant decline, from $71.8 million in school year 1986-87, to $22.5 million in 1990-91, and to

---

[28] Report of the Association of Physical Plant Administrators of Universities and Colleges and National Association of College University Business Officers in Cooperation with Coopers and Lybrand. The Decaying American Campus: A Ticking Time Bomb. Alexandria, VA, 1989. p. 11-55.

[29] U.S. Congress. Senate. Committee on the Budget. Historically Black Colleges and Universities in Higher Education. Testimony of Thomas W. Cole, Jr., President, Clark Atlanta University. Field Hearings. Atlanta, Georgia. 101st Cong., 1st Sess. Washington, U.S. Govt. Print. Off., 1989. p. 134; and U.S. Congress. House. Committee on Science, Space, and Technology. Subcommittee on Science, Research and Technology. Hearing, 100th Cong., 1st Sess. Washington, U.S. Govt. Print. Off., 1987. p. 102-103.

[30] Ibid.

[31] As stated in note 23, caution should be exercised in reviewing the data. Because of the relatively small number of HBCUs, data from a few institutions can skew the quantitative findings and have an effect on the resulting analysis. Scientific and Engineering Research Facilities at Universities and Colleges: 1992, op. cit., p. 6-2.

the expected $11.1 million in school year 1992-93.[32] However,a significant amount of the construction occurred at one or two of the institutions, and as a consequence, the decrease in total construction was not indicative of the entire sample.

An additional analysis of the 29 HBCUs revealed a decline in Federal funding for research facility construction.[33] During the period, 1990-91, HBCUs received approximately $12.1 million in Federal funding, 53.7 percent of these institutions total support, but only 2.5 percent of the total Federal contributions to research facility construction at institutions of higher education. Table 3 below details the source for research facility funding of the sample of 29 HBCUs.

TABLE 3.
Source of Funds for Science/Engineering Research Facilities at Historically Black Colleges and Universities: 1986-91[a]
(dollars in millions)

Funding Source	Construction			Repair/Renovation		
	1986+87	1988+89	1990+91	1986+87	1988+89	1990+91
Federal Government	$32.7	$35.0	$12.1	$8.7	$12.9	$3.5
State/Local Government	25.8	11.5	6.3	4.9	0.8	8.0
Private Donations	11.1	7.7	0.0	0.5	2.0	0.1
Institutional Funds	2.3	0.9	4.2	0.0	0.1	0.1
Total	$71.8	$55.1	$22.5	$14.1	$15.8	$11.6

[a] Scientific and Engineering Research Facilities at Universities and Colleges: 1992, op. cit., p. 6-5.

---

[32] Ibid., p. 6-3.

[33] Declines have been reported also in the other two major sources of funding --State/local government and private donations.

VARIOUS AGENCY SET-ASIDES FOR SUPPORT OF RESEARCH AT HBCUs[34]

P.L. 101-510, The National Defense Authorization Act 1991 (Section 832, Enhancing Participation of Historically Black Colleges and Universities and Minority Institutions in Defense Research), has established a goal of 5 percent for the awarding of prime contracts and subcontracts to HBCUs and other minority institutions to increase their participation " . . . in the performance of defense research and in scientific disciplines critical to the national security functions of the Department of Defense."[35] As an outgrowth of this legislation and in response to the Annual Defense Critical Technologies Plan of the DOD, 14 HBCUS and 7 midwestern research universities established the University Consortium for Research and Development (UCRD). This consortium (seven mini-consortia of three schools each) resulted from a recognized ". . . need for new approaches to inter-university research in the DOD critical technology area, expanded knowledge and personnel in critical technology areas, and enhanced HBCU R&D activity."[36] (As yet, no figures are available for funding levels).[37]

---

[34] There has been no attempt to make this a definitive compilation of Federal agency support, but merely to illustrate the various efforts to address the cumulative effects of limited research infrastructure at HBCUs. Many of the programs in the various agencies were an outgrowth of Executive Orders 12232 and 12320.

[35] Matching funds are required. U.S. Congress. House. Committee of Conference. National Defense Authorization Act for Fiscal Year 1991. Conference Report to Accompany H.R. 4739 (H. Rept. 101-923). 101st Cong., 2d. Sess., Oct. 23, 1990. Washington, U.S. Govt. Print. Off., 1990. p. 133-134.

Minority institutions, other than HBCUs, are defined as those institutions whose enrollments are: (a) more than 50 percent of a combination of any of the following groups: Alaskan Native (Eskimo or Aleut), American Indian, Afro/American Black, Hispanic, or Native Pacific Islander; or (b) 20 percent or more of any one of the above eligible minorities. See section 322(2) of the Higher Education Act of 1965 (20 U.S.C. 1061(2).

[36] U.S. Dept. of Education. White House Initiative for Historically Black Colleges and Universities. Program Prospectus for the Establishment of the University Consortium for Research and Development. Spring, 1991. p. 1.

[37] White House Initiative on Historically Black Colleges. Telephone Interview. Apr. 1, 1993. The consortium members are Alabama A&M University, Clark Atlanta University, Delaware University, Florida A&M University, Hampton University, Howard University, Jackson State University, Indiana University, Iowa State University, North Carolina A&T University, Ohio State University, Prairie View A&M University, Purdue University, Tennessee State University, Texas Southern University, Tuskegee University, University of Arkansas at Pine Bluff, University of Minnesota, University of Missouri, University of Wisconsin, and Xavier University.

P.L. 102-325, the Higher Education Amendments of 1992, provides authority for loans for repair and renovation of academic research facilities, among other facilities. Language in Title VII, Part B, Historically Black Colleges and University Capital Financing (Section 724) of the Higher Education Act as amended (PL 102-325), authorizes establishment of a "designated bonding authority" to raise capital to be lent to HBCUs for repair and renovation of facilities. The aggregate authority principal of these loans cannot be more than $250 million for private HBCUS and no more than $125 million for public HBCUs. At present, this program is not operational.

The U.S. Department of Agriculture, Cooperate State Research Service (CSRS), administers a Capacity Building Grants Program to assist the 1890 land-grant institutions and Tuskegee University strengthen their research and teaching capabilities in high priority areas of the food and agricultural sciences. (These activities includes obtaining state-of-the-art scientific instrumentation for laboratories). For fiscal year 1993, $10.3 million has been appropriated for this program.[38] In addition to the Capacity Building Grants Program, the CSRS provides funding for research at the 1890 institutions through the Evan-Allen formula. Funding for this program for fiscal year 1993 is $27.4 million.

The National Aeronautics and Space Administration (NASA) has initiated a program at seven HBCUs to provide research projects in space science and applications, advanced space technology, and advanced astronautics technology.[39] These institutions will share in approximately $45 to $50 million research grants, dispensed over a period of five years. NASA has supported a total of 40 HBCUs over the years, however, individual grants awarded averaged $75,000 to $100,000. Samuel E. Massenberg, director of NASA's division of minority research and education describes this larger grant program as being: ". . . a heavy investment in infrastructure at black schools . . . designed to help end the underrepresentation of minorities in the sciences."[40]

The NSF has a set-aside of approximately 12 percent of its Academic Research Infrastructure Program for HBCUs and minority institutions.[41] (The

---

[38] Some matching funds are required. For expanded discussion of the 1890 Capacity Building Grants Program, see for example, U.S. Dept. of Agriculture. Agricultural Research. ARS Helps Science Flourish at 1890 Schools, v. 41, Feb. 1993. p. 4-10.

[39] The seven institutions receiving the grants are Howard University, Clark Atlanta University, Fisk University, Hampton University, North Carolina A&T State University, Tuskegee University, and Florida A&M University.

[40] Historically Black Colleges To Aid in NASA Research. Washington Post, June 4, 1992. Metro Section. p. 8.

[41] This 12 percent set-aside was included in the fiscal year 1988 NSF authorization. The program consists of two components: instrumentation and facilities modernization. Matching funds are required.

fiscal year 1993 estimate for program outlays is $50 million). Additional support is provided for research at HBCUs in the NSF's Minority Research Centers of Excellence (MRCEs). Currently the NSF supports eight MRCEs for five years, at a funding level of $5 million for each center.[42]

RECENT COURT RULING EFFECTING HBCUs

In *United States vs. Fordice*, the first ruling on racial segregation in higher education (since *Brown vs. the Board of Education*), the status of all HBCUs would be effected.[43] The Supreme Court ruled that Mississippi had failed to dismantle its current system of higher education. The Court determined that four areas of the Mississippi higher education system were "constitutionally suspect" (admission standards, program duplication at the historically black and white colleges, assigned missions for the institutions, and the question of whether the State should continue operation of all eight public colleges). The Supreme Court ordered the U.S. District Court in Mississippi to review the four areas. In response, to the ruling, the Mississippi Board of Trustees of Institutions of Higher Learning proposed closing one HBCU and merging another with a predominantly white institution. The proposal also included closing the only schools of veterinary medicine and dentistry in the State (both predominantly white) and developing "contractual relationships" with out-of-State institutions for students in these disciplines.[44]

While some in the legal and academic communities viewed the decision with cautious optimism, others maintained that the ruling would spur considerable litigation. Academicians, who had been fighting to maintain and strengthen the infrastructure of HBCUs, contend that black colleges in many States would be vulnerable to closing. Still others believe that the impact of the

---

[42] For expanded discussion of these centers, see Matthews, *supra* note 17.

[43] The ruling on June 26, 1992, extended the application of *Brown vs. Board of Education* to higher education. For discussion of the U.S. Supreme Court's opinion and dissenting opinion see for example, Supreme Court of the United States. Black Issues in Higher Education, v. 9, July 16, 1992. p. 26-49, Mercer, Joye. Black-College Officials Share Disillusionment Over Supreme Court Desegregation Ruling. The Chronicle of Higher Education, v. 39, Oct. 28, 1992. p. A34; and Implications of Mississippi Higher Education Desegregation. Educational Record, v. 74, Spring 1993. p. 56-57.

[44] The Louisiana Board of Regents has approved a similar desegregation plan in which the only historically black college system would be dismantled. Mercer, Joye. La. Desegregation Plan Would Break Up Higher-Education Systems. The Chronicle of Higher Education, v. 39, Dec. 16, 1991. p. A24.

decision would not be realized until it was interpreted by the lower courts and applied by the states.[46]

CONCLUSIONS

The viability of any academic institution is a function of its ability to provide a quality education for its student population. Data reveal that many HBCUs have provided their black student population with a quality education, especially in the scientific and technical disciplines. However, these institutions are faced with an added challenge of attracting and preparing an increasingly larger number of blacks in the sciences. Demographic data show a student population and workforce increasingly composed of minorities (blacks and Hispanics), groups that have been historically underrepresented in the sciences. This demographic pattern may affect the development of the scientific and engineering workforce and, consequently, the conduct of R&D in the 21st century. The success of research programs at HBCUs is inextricably linked to their ability to provide an environment for fostering additional scientific talent.

The distribution of Federal funding for HBCUs is one of the critical issues facing these institutions. Many HBCUs encounter difficulty competing for scarce research dollars with major research universities. For the most part, past and current policies have not provided effective remedies for their problems of infrastructure necessary to develop strong scientific programs. While many HBCUs have engaged in strategic planning in order to maintain and obtain a competitive research base, Congress may continue to consider options that would bring HBCUs closer to an equal footing with other institutions and enable them to be full partners in conducting research. The issue of strengthening the capacity of minority institutions could not only contribute to the long-term health of the Nation's higher education system, but could assist in producing an increasingly larger number of trained scientific and technical personnel needed to meet the challenge of a highly competitive international economy.

---

[46] See for example, Matthews, Frank L. Ultimate Impact of Ayers Case Depends on Many Factors. Black Issues in Higher Education, v. 9, July 16, 1992. p. 1, 26; Halpern, Stephen C. A Bedeviling and Worrisome Court Ruling on Black Colleges. The Chronicle of Higher Education, v. 39, Nov. 4, 1992. p. B1-B2; Mercer, Joye. Plan to Desegregate Higher Education in Mississippi Unites State's Colleges, Black and White Alike. The Chronicle of Higher Education, v. 39, Nov. 4, 1992. p. A23-A24; Jaschik, Scott. High-Court Ruling Transforms Battles Over Desegregation at Colleges in 19 States. The Chronicle of Higher Education, v. 39, July 8, 1992. p. A16-A18; and Jaschik, Scott and Joye Mercer. Public Black Colleges Face New Pressures. The Chronicle of Higher Education, v. 38, July 15, 1992. p. A21-A23.

TABLE A. 1890 Land-Grant Institutions
Alabama A&M University
University of Arkansas, Pine Bluff
Delaware State College
Florida A&M University
Fort Valley State College
Kentucky State University
Souther University, Louisiana
University of Maryland, Eastern Shore
Alcorn State University
Lincoln University, Missouri
North Carolina A&T State University
Langston State University
South Carolina State College
Tennessee State University
Prairie View A&M University
Virginia State University
Tuskegee University
University of the District of Columbia
University of the Virgin Islands, St. Thomas Campus

TABLE B.
1990 Fall Enrollment in Historically Black Colleges and Universities, by Institution and Type of Control

Institution	State	Year Established	Type of Control	Fall 1990 Enrollment[a]
Alabama A&M University	AL	1875	Public 4-year	4,886
Alabama State University	AL	1874	Public 4-year	4,587
Bishop State Community College	AL	1927	Public 2-year	2,057
C.A. Fredd State Technical College	AL	1965	Public 2-year	279
Carver State Technical College	AL	1962	Public 2-year	535
Concordia College	AL	1922	Private 2-year	380
J.F. Drake Technical College	AL	1961	Public 2-year	852
Lawson State Community College	AL	1965	Public 2-year	1,711
Miles College	AL	1905	Private 4-year	584
Oakwood College	AL	1896	Private 4-year	1,266
Selma University	AL	1878	Private 4-year	316
Stillman College	AL	1876	Private 4-year	770
Talladega College	AL	1867	Private 4-year	667
Trenholm State Technical College	AL	1966	Public 2-year	783
Tuskegee University	AL	1881	Private 4-year	3,510

TABLE B. (continued)
1990 Fall Enrollment in Historically Black Colleges and Universities, by Institution and Type of Control

Institution	State	Year Established	Type of Control	Fall 1990 Enrollment
Arkansas Baptist College	AR	1901	Private 4-year	291
Philander Smith College	AR	1877	Private 4-year	594
Shorter College	AR	1886	Private 2-year	135
University of Arkansas, Pine Bluff	AR	1873	Public 4-year	3,672
Delaware State College	DE	1891	Public 4-year	2,606
Howard University[b]	DC	1867	Private 4-year	11,617
University of the District of Columbia[c]	DC	1851[d]	Public 4-year	11,990
Bethune-Cookman College	FL	1904	Private 4-year	2,342
Edward Waters College	FL	1866	Private 4-year	597
Florida A&M University	FL	1877	Private 4-year	8,344
Florida Memorial College	FL	1879	Public 4-year	2,251
Albany State College	GA	1903	Public 4-year	2,405
Clark Atlanta University[e]	GA	1989	Private 4-year	3,508
Fort Valley State College	GA	1895	Public 4-year	2,158
Interdenominational Theological Center	GA	1958	Private 4-year	294

TABLE B. (continued)
1990 Fall Enrollment in Historically Black Colleges and Universities, by Institution and Type of Control

Institution	State	Year Established	Type of Control	Fall 1990 Enrollment
Morehouse College	GA	1867	Private 4-year	2,720
Morehouse School of Medicine	GA	1978	Private 4-year	145
Morris Brown College	GA	1881	Private 4-year	2,049
Paine College	GA	1882	Private 4-year	606
Savannah State College	GA	1890	Public 4-year	2,319
Spelman College	GA	1881	Private 4-year	1,710
Kentucky State University	KY	1886	Public 4-year	2,506
Dillard University	LA	1869	Private 4-year	1,998
Grambling State University	LA	1901	Public 4-year	6,485
Southern University and A&M College, Baton Rouge	LA	1880	Public 4-year	8,941
Southern University, New Orleans	LA	1959	Public 4-year	4,064
Southern University, Shreveport-Bossier City Campus	LA	1964	Public 2-year	1,020
Xavier University of Louisiana	LA	1915	Private 4-year	2,943
Bowie State University	MD	1865	Public 4-year	4,188

TABLE B. (continued)
1990 Fall Enrollment in Historically Black Colleges and Universities, by Institution and Type of Control

Institution	State	Year Established	Type of Control	Fall 1990 Enrollment
Coppin State College	MD	1900	Public 4-year	2,578
Morgan State University	MD	1867	Public 4-year	4,693
University of Maryland, Eastern Shore	MD	1886	Public 4-year	2,067
Lewis College of Business	MI	1874	Private 2-year	233
Alcorn State University	MS	1871	Public 4-year	2,863
Coahoma Community College	MS	1949	Public 2-year	1,351
Hinds Community College, Utica Campus	MS	1954	Public 2-year	668
Jackson State University	MS	1877	Public 4-year	6,837
Mary Holmes College	MS	1892	Private 2-year	742
Mississippi Valley State University	MS	1946	Public 4-year	1,873
Rust College	MS	1866	Private 4-year	1,021
Tougaloo College	MS	1869	Private 4-year	956

TABLE B. (continued)
1990 Fall Enrollment in Historically Black Colleges and Universities, by Institution and Type of Control

Institution	State	Year Established	Type of Control	Fall 1990 Enrollment
Harris-Stowe State College	MO	1857	Public 4-year	1,973
Lincoln University	MO	1866	Public 4-year	3,619
Barber-Scotia College	NC	1867	Private 4-year	422
Bennett College	NC	1873	Private 4-year	586
Elizabeth City State University	NC	1891	Public 4-year	1,746
Fayetteville State University	NC	1877	Public 4-year	3,337
Johnson C. Smith University	NC	1867	Private 4-year	1,182
Livingstone College	NC	1879	Private 4-year	682
North Carolina A&T State University	NC	1891	Public 4-year	6,595
North Carolina Central University	NC	1910	Public 4-year	5,482
St. Augustine's College	NC	1867	Private 4-year	1,900
Shaw University	NC	1865	Private 4-year	1,846
Winston-Salem State University	NC	1892	Public 4-year	2,517
Central State University	OH	1887	Public 4-year	2,886
Wilberforce University	OH	1856	Private 4-year	809

TABLE B. (continued)
1990 Fall Enrollment in Historically Black Colleges and Universities, by Institution and Type of Control

Institution	State	Year Established	Type of Control	Fall 1990 Enrollment
Langston University	OK	1897	Public 4-year	2,792
Cheyney University of Pennsylvania	PA	1837	Public 4-year	1,738
Lincoln University	PA	1854	Public 4-year	1,374
Allen University	SC	1870	Private 4-year	233
Benedict College	SC	1870	Private 4-year	1,478
Clinton Junior College	SC	1894	Private 2-year	88
Claflin College	SC	1869	Private 4-year	913
Denmark Technical College	SC	1948	Public 2-year	617
Morris College	SC	1908	Private 4-year	760
South Carolina State College	SC	1896	Public 4-year	4,822
Voorhees College	SC	1897	Private 4-year	566
Fisk University	TN	1867	Private 4-year	911
Knoxville College	TN	1875	Private 4-year	1,266
Lane College	TN	1882	Private 4-year	530
Le Moyne-Owen College	TN	1862	Private 4-year	1,066

TABLE B. (continued)
1990 Fall Enrollment in Historically Black Colleges and Universities, by Institution and Type of Control

Institution	State	Year Established	Type of Control	Fall 1990 Enrollment
Meharry Medical College	TN	1876	Private 4-year	623
Tennessee State University	TN	1912	Public 4-year	7,393
Huston-Tillotson College	TX	1876	Private 4-year	714
Jarvis Christian College	TX	1912	Private 4-year	598
Paul Quinn College	TX	1872	Private 4-year	997
Prairie View A&M University	TX	1876	Public 4-year	4,990
St. Phillip's College	TX	1927	Public 2-year	5,204
Southwestern Christian College	TX	1949	Private 4-year	225
Texas College	TX	1894	Private 4-year	478
Texas Southern University	TX	1947	Public 4-year	9,427
Wiley College	TX	1873	Private 4-year	463
Hampton University	VA	1868	Private 4-year	5,305
Norfolk State University	VA	1935	Public 4-year	8,008
St. Paul's College	VA	1888	Private 4-year	574
Virginia State University	VA	1882	Public 4-year	3,988
Virginia Union University	VA	1865	Private 4-year	1,298

TABLE B. (continued)
1990 Fall Enrollment in Historically Black Colleges and Universities, by Institution and Type of Control

Institution	State	Year Established	Type of Control	Fall 1990 Enrollment
Bluefield State College	WV	1895	Public 4-year	2,702
West Virginia State College	WV	1891	Public 4-year	4,834
University of the Virgin Islands, St. Thomas Campus	VI	1962	Public 4-year	1,684

[a] In the absence of reported enrollment data from some institutions, the Department of Education made estimations based on previous year enrollments.

[b] Howard University is the only HBCU classified by the Carnegie Foundation as "Research University I."

[c] See above note.

[d] The University of the District of Columbia (UDC) is the only metropolitan land-grant institution of higher education. UDC was formed in 1976 with the merger of D.C. Teachers College (founded in 1851 as Miner's Teacher College), Federal City College, and Washington Technical Institute.

[e] Atlanta University and Clark College merged in July 1989 and became Clark Atlanta University.

Black Americans:
Issues and Concerns

ISBN 1-56072-173-1

THE VOTING RIGHTS ACT OF 1965, AS AMENDED: ITS HISTORY AND CURRENT ISSUES*

G.P. Laney

SUMMARY

This report analyzes key provisions of the Voting Rights Act of 1965 and its amendments of 1970, 1975 and 1982. It discusses arguments in support of and against the extension of Section 203 of the Act.

Congress passed the Voting Rights Act of 1965 in response to widespread evidence of disfranchisement of black citizens in several southern States. This Act protects citizens' right to vote primarily by forbidding these States from using tests of any kind to determine eligibility to vote, by requiring these States to obtain Federal approval before enacting any election laws, and by assigning Federal officials to monitor the registration process in certain localities.

* Excerpted from CIS Report 92-578.

In 1970, the Federal Government continued the Voting Rights Act for an additional five years, and extended its coverage to other jurisdictions when evidence presented at congressional hearings revealed that racial discrimination in voting was continuing. Coverage of the Act was extended to the entire country instead of just southern States. A nationwide ban on all literacy tests for voter registrants was added. Amendments addressed residency requirements for voting in Federal elections.

The Voting Rights Act was amended again in 1975. Congress continued the Act for seven more years. Some members of the Hispanic community related voting experiences to Congress that paralleled those of blacks. In response, Congress extended coverage of the Act to more jurisdictions to protect the voting rights of ethnic groups whose language is other than English, and added provisions to the Act that require bilingual election assistance for voters who need it. The Act permanently prohibits the use of literacy tests for voter registration. The Act also provides that the Census Bureau compile registration and voting statistics.

In 1982, Congress amended the Act by expanding the conditions required for release from coverage. Congress extended the required period for compliance with the Act under Section 4(a). The amendments provide that Congress "reconsider" the administrative provisions of the Act (preclearance of election-law changes and assignment of examiners and election observers) in 1997, and that these provisions shall expire in 2007. The amendments enable courts to judge an election law to be discriminatory without proof that it was intended to be so, if the law resulted in abridging minority voting power.

The current issues before the 102nd Congress include whether to extend the bilingual election provisions of Section 203 that presently terminate on August 6, 1992, whether to clarify coverage of Sections 2 and 5, and whether to cover additional expenses of litigants.

INTRODUCTION

Right to Vote

Prior to the Civil War, the franchise was denied to nearly everyone except white male property owners who were over 21 years of age. After the War, during the Reconstruction period, however, Congress, with passage of the First Reconstruction Act of 1867, required former confederate states to write new constitutions that guaranteed the right of all males to vote, irrespective of race. Also in 1867, the 15th Amendment was adopted, which protected the right of male suffrage without regard to "race, color, or previous condition of servitude." From 1867 to 1875, Congress passed election laws that guaranteed the right to vote in national and State elections and established Federal supervision of election and voter registration. To protect the political, legal and social equality of all Americans, Congress passed civil rights legislation that contained provisions for the imposition of fines and criminal penalties on those convicted of conspiring to deprive citizens of their civil rights. As a consequence of these laws, black participation in the political process rose dramatically. For example, during this period nearly 70 percent of the eligible black voters were registered; ten blacks were elected to the House and two to the U.S. Senate. Besides electing blacks to office, black voters heavily influenced the outcome of local, State and national elections throughout the South.[1]

Most southern whites opposed the enfranchisement of former slaves. Soon they resorted to a number of tactics to discourage or stop blacks from participating in the political process, such as fraud, violence (including murder), and economic blackmail. The Compromise of 1877 essentially ended Reconstruction, as withdrawal of Federal troops from the South allowed those who supported the disfranchisement of blacks to assume control of most State governments. These legislatures used creative measures to make voting difficult. They passed bills to reduce the numbers of black voters by requiring them to travel great distances to voting precincts and designed complex balloting procedures that virtually amounted to literacy tests. All challenges to

---

[1]U.S. Congress. House. Committee on the Judiciary. Subcommittee #5, Voting Rights. Hearings on H.R. 6400. 89th Congress, 1st session. Wshington, U.S. Govt. Print. Off., 1965, p. 3-4; U.S. Congress. Senate. Committee on the Judiciary. Subcommittee on the Constitution. Voting Rights Act. Report. 97th Congress, 2d session. Washington, U.S. Govt. Print. Off., 1982 (at head of title: committee print). p. 7; Franklin, John Hope. *From Slavery to Freedom: A History of Negro Americans*. New York, Alfred A. Knopf, 1980, p. 242-50.

registration rulings were heard by local officials who were unlikely to be sympathetic.[2]

A South Carolina law of 1882 required that special ballots and boxes be placed in every polling place for each office on the ballot, and that voters put their ballots in the correct boxes. No one was allowed to speak to a voter, and if he failed to find the correct box, his vote was thrown out.[3] All of these tactics—both legal and illegal—combined to do what they were designed to do—minimize the presence of blacks in the electoral process. Those Southern whites who were uncomfortable with the resort to fraud, murder, bribery and theft sought a permanent legal way to disfranchise blacks.[4]

Constitutional Disfranchisement

During the last decade of the nineteenth century, a number of southern States held constitutional conventions to permanently disfranchise black Americans. Although delegates at these conventions favored repeal of the 15th Amendment, they feared the reaction of the rest of the Nation. They need not have though, for the political climate of the country, both North and South, seemed to favor limiting black participation in the political process (for different reasons of course). Federal enforcement of election laws and protection of citizens was being withdrawn. The Supreme Court, in 1883, narrowly interpreted provisions of civil rights laws passed during Reconstruction or declared them unconstitutional. Congress repealed many sections of the Enforcement Act. These rulings effectively removed the Federal Government from the business of protecting the civil rights of all Americans for over fifty years.[5]

At its constitutional convention of 1890 (called for the express purpose of removing blacks from the ballot box), Mississippi devised a system that permanently disfranchised blacks and served as a model for the rest of the South. Because delegates at the convention feared voters would reject the new constitution, they did not submit it for popular approval, instead the convention, itself, approved, promulgated and declared the constitution to be in effect. The Mississippi constitution of 1890 differed from the old in that it replaced the six months residency requirement with a two-years one; imposed a literacy test for prospective voters, as well as a property requirement of three hundred dollars; introduced an annual poll tax of two dollars; and disqualified convicts.[6]

---

[2]Franklin, *From Slavery to Freedom*, p. 255-58, 263-67.

[3]Ibid., p. 259-60.

[4]Ibid., p. 258-63.

[5]Ibid., p. 255-58.

[6]Ibid., p. 263-64.

Virginia's election code in 1894 required that registration and poll tax certificates be shown at the polls, and that the names of candidates be printed on the ballot by *office* not party. This was a confusing arrangement for barely literate and illiterate voters. Voters had a maximum of two and a half minutes to vote, if others were waiting in line. As a consequence of this code both black and white illiterate residents were disfranchised.[7]

In 1898, Louisiana introduced a new device into its constitution, the "grandfather clause." It required an addition to the permanent registration list of the names of all male persons whose fathers and grandfathers were qualified to vote on January 1, 1867. Since blacks were denied the franchise in 1867, none of them qualified under this provision. The Supreme Court in 1915 declared the "grandfather clause" unconstitutional.[8]

All but two Southern States used literacy tests as the heart of their disfranchisement schemes; however, none of the new constitutional provisions mentioned race, i.e., they were racially neutral. But the impact of these laws was devastating for blacks. For instance, in Mississippi, in 1867, 70 percent of eligible blacks were registered to vote; by 1889, only 9 percent. In Louisiana, in 1896, 130,334 blacks were registered to vote, by 1900, only 5,320. Alabama in 1900 had 181,471 black males of voting age, but after the new constitution was adopted only 3,000 registered.[9]

Early Supreme Court Cases

For decades these laws were enforced. Eleven Southern States determined that the state political party nominating process was a private action and, therefore, that party officials could legally restrict participation in the primary to whites only (thus the name "white primary"). Since the winner of the primary in a one-party State, was in essence elected to office, African Americans were eliminated from the electoral process.[10] A suit was filed in Texas, *Smith v. Allwright*,[11] challenging the constitutionality of the white primary; in 1944, the Supreme Court declared the white primary unconstitutional.

---

[7]Ibid., p. 259.

[8]Greenberg, Jack, *Race Relations and American Law*, New York, Columbia University Press, 1959, p. 139.

[9]Ibid., p. 264-67; Gurin, Patricia, Shirley Hatchett, and James S. Jackson, *Hope and Independence, Blacks' Response to Electoral and Party Politics*, New York, Russell Sage Foundation, 1989, p. 23.

[10]Bass, Jack, *Unlikely Heroes*, Simon and Schuster, New York, p. 266.

[11]321 U.S. 649 (1944).

Nonetheless, Southern legislatures developed other means to deny blacks access to the voting booth. In July 1957, the Alabama legislature with Act No. 140 redrew the boundaries of the city of Tuskegee to keep thousands of black residents and nearly all blacks who were registered to vote from participating in elections. A resident, Charles G. Gomillion, in *Gomillion v. Lightfoot*[12] charged that the Act violated both the 14th Amendment (the equal protection clause) and the 15th Amendment. This was an important case because two issues were involved—voting rights for blacks and redistricting by State legislatures.[13]

In the past, Supreme Court rulings appeared to give State legislatures absolute control over setting municipal boundaries. In 1957, as the Court began to dismantle barriers to black political participation, it considered the redistricting issue inherent in *Gomillion v. Lightfoot*. Although Act No. 140 did not mention race, it was clear that its intent was racially discriminatory. Yet, on appeal, the Fifth Circuit Court of Appeals, by a 3-2 vote, upheld a lower court's dismissal of the case on the grounds that it lacked "authority or jurisdiction" to declare the law void. But dissenting Judge John Brown noted that the fact that Act No. 140 did not discriminate on its face was insignificant; the act "effectively disfranchised all but four or five black voters."[14] Brown also considered the fact that the State legislature in trying to abolish the county in which Tuskegee was located had not established a board of registrars. Since most eligible whites were already registered, they had no real need for a registrar. But thousands of blacks were not registered and were unable to register to vote for lack of a board of registrars. Therefore, the traditional method of correcting political abuse at the polls was denied blacks. Consequently, Judge Brown found the law unconstitutional. He wrote that "the business of judging in constitutional fields is one of searching for the spirit of the Constitution in terms of the present as well as the past, not the past alone." On appeal, the Supreme Court agreed with Judge Brown and ruled unanimously that Act No. 140 violated the 15th amendment.[15]

---

[12]270 F. 2d 594, 611.

[13]Bass, *Unlikely Heroes*, p. 97-100.

[14]Ibid, p. 107.

[15]Ibid., p. 106-109.

Civil Rights Acts of 1957, 1960 and 1964

In 1957, Congress passed the Civil Rights Act to protect black voting rights through the judicial process. By provisions of the Act, the Attorney General was authorized to bring lawsuits to protect equal voting rights, and persons who disobeyed court orders prohibiting discrimination in voting could be held in criminal contempt. Moreover, the Act authorized appointment of another Assistant Attorney General to head a Civil Rights Division in the Department of Justice. It provided that special three-judge Federal district courts be convened, with jurisdiction to hear civil rights cases taken out of State courts by the Department of Justice. A six-member Commission on Civil Rights was created to gather information on discrimination in voting and to issue annual reports.[16]

The Commission on Civil Rights held hearings throughout the Nation and discovered that some registrars discriminated against blacks for racial reasons. Because of the length of legal hearings and all of the delaying but legal tactics employed during lawsuits, the Civil Rights Act of 1957 was mostly ineffective. After three years only four cases were heard and decided. It was felt that the law needed strengthening to prevent evasive measures by registrars and produce more timely rulings; so in 1960, Congress passed another Civil Rights law.

The Civil Rights Act of 1960 sought to fill some of the loopholes in the 1957 Act. It provided that if a registrar resigned after complaints had been filed, the proceeding could be instituted against the State. It authorized Federal referees to investigate complaints of voting discrimination and to register qualified voters. The Act required voting records to be preserved for twenty-two months following any primary, special, or general election at which there were candidates for Federal office; and it empowered a Federal district court judge to issue a registration order, and to replace State registrars with Federal officials.[17]

But these measures proved inadequate because the individual black citizen, operating in a hostile environment, had to be the primary initiator of legal action. In a report prepared in 1963, the Commission on Civil Rights concluded that this was a role that the Federal Government should assume. Federal efforts to ban racial discrimination relied heavily on litigation. The Commission rejected this approach because it was time consuming and did not increase black registration significantly.

National political leaders remained committed to a low-profile approach based on litigation to registering blacks in the South until violence erupted in Birmingham, Alabama, in 1963 and Philadelphia, Mississippi, in 1964. In response to the violence, Congress passed the Civil Rights Act of 1964, which

---

[16]P.L. 83-315; 71 Stat. 634.

[17]P.L. 86-449; 74 Stat. 86.

contains provisions that attempted to have three-judge Federal district courts hear cases more quickly, and allow for temporary voting registrars. It forbids local officials to apply standards to some voter registrants (e.g., black registrants) that had not been applied to others (e.g., white registrants) already found qualified to vote. The Act also provides that in any voting rights court case there shall be a presumption of literacy for all voter applicants who have completed the sixth grade in an accredited, English-speaking school. These provisions proved ineffective as well. Sometimes, after lengthy litigation caused an election law to be judicially invalidated as discriminatory, the State or local jurisdiction would pass and enforce a different law or regulation designed to circumvent the court order. In drafting another voting rights bill, the Justice Department called for a "new approach" that would go "beyond the tortuous, often-ineffective pace of litigation."[18] It sought to impose constraints on the use of literacy tests and other devices that denied blacks access to the ballot box, and to establish an administrative presence of Federal marshals in the southern States to assist blacks in their efforts to vote. The outbreak of violence in Selma, Alabama, as a result of a black voter registration drive, aided the Department in its efforts. On August 6, 1965, the Voting Rights Act was signed into law.[19] It created administrative remedies that automatically became applicable to certain jurisdictions under a statutory coverage formula, without the need for prolonged litigation. In *South Carolina v Katzenbach,*[20] the Supreme Court upheld the constitutionality of the Voting Rights Act.

---

[18]House Subcommittee No. 5, p. 5, 9.

[19]P.L. 89-110; 79 Stat. 437.

[20]383 U.S. 301 (1966)

THE VOTING RIGHTS ACT OF 1965 (P.L. 89-110)

Congress passed the Voting Rights Act to protect the voting rights of American citizens. The Act was amended in 1970, 1975 and 1982.[21]

Major provisions of the Voting Rights Act of 1965:

1) Prohibit the enactment of any election law to deny or abridge voting rights on account of race or color;
2) Suspend all literacy tests in States and counties that used them and where less than 50 percent of adults had voted in 1964;
3) Prohibit the enforcement of new voting rules or practices until Federal reviewers determine if their use would continue voting discrimination;
4) Assign Federal examiners to list qualified applicants to vote and to serve as poll watchers; and
5) Authorize the Attorney General to institute civil actions to seek enforcement of the Act.

Coverage Formula (Section 4(b))

Justification for Federal intervention in State regulation of the electoral process restricted intervention to jurisdictions in which there was evidence that voting discrimination had occurred. A coverage formula was adopted to determine which States and political subdivisions of States would be covered by the Act. It was assumed that low registration and voting statistics in jurisdictions requiring literacy tests and devices resulted from the discriminatory application of those tests and devices. Therefore, according to the formula established in Section 4(b), any States or political subdivisions are covered if

---

[21]In order to provide a more logical order of presentation, the following summary does not follow the numerical sequence of sections of the Voting Rights Act. Thus, the summary rearranges the subject matter as follows: first, the rationale for deciding which jurisdictions are to be subject to the Act; second, the requirements imposed on covered jurisdictions; third, how these jurisdictions may be released from coverage. Other sections of the Act are placed after these. As a result of this rearrangement, parts of the Act in Title I are taken up after parts in Titles II and III. In order to avoid confusion, title numbers have been omitted. Sections numbered below 200 are in Title I; those in the 200's are in Title II; and those in the 300's are in Title III. The summary includes only the fundamental sections of the Act; other sections are omitted.

they used any test or device as a condition for voter registration on November 1, 1964, and if either less than 50 percent of age-eligible persons living there were registered to vote on that date or less than 50 percent of such persons voted in the Presidential election of that year.[22]

Suspension of Tests and Devices (Section 4(a))

The Act forbids the use of all literacy tests as well as any other "device," such as a voucher requirement, as a condition for voter registration in States and political subdivisions of States that fall under the coverage criteria of Section 4(b).

Preclearance of Changes in Election Laws (Section 5)

With Section 4(a) the framers of the Voting Rights Act sought to stop the practice of discouraging black registration and voting. But they also realized that covered jurisdictions could limit the effectiveness of the black vote in other ways, for instance, by locating polling places in white but not in black neighborhoods, and by gerrymandering electoral districts in such a way that blacks would not comprise a majority in any electoral district. Section 5 is intended to prevent enforcement of any discriminatory election law made after November 1, 1964.[23]

The Act prohibits a covered State or political subdivision from putting into effect "any voting qualification or prerequisite to voting, or standard, practice, or procedure with respect to voting different from that in force or effect on November 1, 1964" before first submitting the change in election law for "preclearance" either to the Justice Department or to the U.S. District Court for the District of Columbia (in an action for a declaratory judgment) in order for the Department or the Court to determine if such law would deny or abridge the right to vote on account of race or color.[24] In order to object to an election law change submitted for Federal preclearance, the Justice Department or the U.S. District Court for the District of Columbia need not find that the jurisdiction *intended* to discriminate against black voters; it need only determine that

---

[22]The following jurisdictions were covered by the "triggering" provisions of Section 4(b) in 1965: Alabama, Georgia, Louisiana, Mississippi, South Carolina, Virginia, 39 counties in North Carolina, and specified counties in Arizona and Hawaii. The Justice Department publishes the list of covered jurisdictions in 28 C.F.R. 51.54, Appendix.

[23]U.S. Congress. House. Committee on Rules. To Extend The Voting Rights Act of 1965 With Respect to the Discriminatory Use of Tests and Devices. Hearings on H.R. 4249. 91st Congress, 1st session. Washington, U.S. Govt. Print. Off., 1969. p. 3. (Statement of Representative Celler, Chairman of the House Judiciary Committee).

[24]42 U.S.C. §1973c.

implementation of the law would, in fact, *result* in denying or abridging voting rights. If the Justice Department does not object to the proposed law within 60 days after a jurisdiction submits it for review, then the jurisdiction may put the law into effect.

Laws Affecting Elections That Require Preclearance

Section 5 requires Federal preclearance of every kind of law affecting elections, not only procedural requirements that individuals must observe in order to register and vote, but laws setting up electoral systems as well. Between 1965 and 1980 (Section 5 was continued when the Act was amended in 1970, 1975 and 1982) in the preclearance process the Justice Department objected more times to three of these ways than to any others—methods of election, urban annexations, and electoral redistricting. These methods were objectionable because they would have resulted in abridging or "diluting" the voting power of blacks, Hispanics or other protected minority voters.

Altering Methods of Election

Changing from single-member districts to at-large voting. One objectionable way of altering the method of election was changing from election by single-member districts or precincts to at-large voting. For example, in a majority-white city governed by several commissioners, if each commissioner were elected in a different district, and if blacks, as a minority in the city as a whole, nevertheless comprised the majority in one or more districts, then black voters would be in a position to elect one or more candidates of their own choice. But, if commissioners were elected at-large, it would usually mean that all voters in the city as a whole would vote for each commissioner position, and consequently, that the white majority in the city as a whole could elect every one of the nine commissioners. Thus, a change in method of election from election by single-member districts to at-large elections would dissolve any black majorities in separate districts and allow the white city-wide majority to decide the entire outcome of elections for the city commission.

It is this kind of "dilution" of black voting power to which the Justice Department often has objected. It should be noted that at-large elections in white-majority jurisdictions are not necessarily discriminatory. However, they may become so in certain circumstances, where racial antagonism and racial bloc voting characterize the jurisdiction or socioeconomic issues such as unemployment or poverty divide a jurisdiction along racial lines.

Urban annexations. The Justice Department found that urban annexations also may abridge black voting power. For instance, if a majority-black city annexed a largely white suburban area, the enlarged city might change from majority-black to majority-white. If the city conducted elections for municipal offices at-large, and if the addition of suburban whites gave whites a city-wide majority, then black voters might lose the chance to elect their own candidates to any municipal office. This development occurred with the annexation of suburban areas by Petersburg, Virginia, in 1971; the black percentage of the population changed from 55 to 46 percent. Because Petersburg conducted at-large elections for the City Council the Justice Department believed that the annexation would have diluted black voting power. Petersburg was allowed to annex suburban areas only on the condition that it change from at-large elections to elections by single-member districts.[25]

Redistricting. Changing the boundaries of single-member electoral districts is another method of altering the method of election that the Justice Department determined may result in lessening the effectiveness of the black vote. In a jurisdiction with concentrations of black voters, such concentrations constitute potential majorities able to elect candidates responsive to the needs of the black community. If district boundaries are drawn to divide concentrations of black voters into adjoining, majority-white areas, black majorities may be liquidated. Conversely, boundaries of single-member electoral districts may be drawn in such a way as to minimize the number of black-majority districts by placing black voters in as few districts as possible.

It has been suggested that implementation of Section 5 by the Justice Department has fostered the expectation that fair electoral processes should result in racially proportional representation among elected officials.[26] That is, blacks should be able to elect officeholders in numbers fairly proportional to the percentage that they comprise of the entire electorate. But Section 5 does not establish a right to proportional representation. Rather, the purpose of preclearance of election law changes is to prevent jurisdictions with a history of discrimination and racial polarization from manipulating the electoral systems to render the black vote ineffective.[27]

Federal Examiners for Voter Registration (Sections 6 and 7)

Whenever the Attorney General receives written complaints of denial of the right to vote for racial reasons from 20 or more residents of a jurisdiction, or whenever the Attorney General thinks it is advisable, Section 6 authorizes the Attorney General to request the U.S. Office of Personnel Management to send Federal examiners to list eligible voters for registration in any political

---

[25]U.S. Commission on Civil Rights. *The Voting Rights Act: Ten Years After.* Washington, U.S. Commission of Civil Rights, 1975. p. 304-5.

[26]Thernstrom, Abigail. "The Odd Evolution of the Voting Rights Act," *The Public Interest*, No. 55, Spring 1979: 49-76.

[27]U.S. Commission on Civil Rights. The Voting Rights Act: Unfulfilled Goals. Washington, U.S. Commission on Civil Rights, 1981, p. 38-42; U.S. Congress. House. Committee on the Judiciary. Voting Rights Extension. Report to Accompany H.R. 3112. 97th Congress, 1st session. H. Rept. 97-227. Washington, U.S. Govt. Print. Off., 1981. p. 17-20.

subdivision of a State if the political subdivision is covered by Section 4(a) (suspension of tests and devices).

Section 7 prescribes procedures for the listing of voter registrants by Federal examiners.

Federal Election Observers (Section 8)

Section 8 authorizes the Attorney General to request the Office of Personnel Management to send election observers to any political subdivision where an examiner has been assigned. Election observers assure that all registered voters are allowed to vote, and that all votes are counted.

Release from Coverage (Section 4(a))

To obtain release from Federal regulations a State or subdivision must obtain a declaratory judgment to the effect that for the preceding five years no literary tests or similar devices were used to deny the right to vote for racial reasons. By 1970, Alaska and counties within Arizona, Idaho and North Carolina were released from the prohibitions of the Act.

Prohibition of English-Language Literacy Requirement for Citizens Educated in American Schools (Section 4(e))

Section 4(e) forbids any American citizen who has successfully completed the sixth grade in any accredited, American-flag school in which the language is other than English from being denied the right to vote because of inability to read, write, or understand the English language. This provision was intended to protect the half-million Puerto Ricans of voting age residing in New York City who had been educated in American schools in Puerto Rico where classroom instruction was entirely in Spanish (as contrasted with bilingual schools). Many could not meet the English-literacy requirement for voting in New York.[28]

General Prohibition of Discriminatory Voting Laws (Section 2)

Section 2 forbids any State or political subdivision to enact any election law "to deny or abridge" voting rights on account of race or color. It is a statutory form of the Fifteenth Amendment, and is a basis for judicial enforcement by court suits.[29] Section 2 is applicable not only to jurisdictions covered through

---

[28]*Congressional Record*, v. 111, part 8: 11060-1.

[29]U.S. Congress. Senate. Committee on the Judiciary. Subcommittee on the Constitution. Voting Rights Act. Report on S. 1992. 97th Congress, 2d session. Washington, U.S. Govt. Print. Off., 1982 (at head of title: committee print). p. 20.

Section 4(b), but applies nationwide. Unlike other sections of the Act, it is a requirement from which jurisdictions cannot be released from coverage after a certain period of time. Moreover, while Section 5 preclearance is limited to changes made in election laws since November 1, 1964, election laws may be challenged in court under Section 2 regardless of when they were enacted.

Prior to its amendment in 1982, the standard for determining whether an election law violated Section 2 differed from the standard applicable in Section 5. The standard for determining violation of Section 2 from 1965 to 1982 was whether the law in question was enacted with the *purpose* or *intention* of abridging voting rights. Because of the difficulty of demonstrating such a violation in court, this standard was changed in 1982, to permit it to be demonstrated that the law in question *resulted* in the abridgment of voting rights.[30]

Civil Actions to Enforce Compliance (Section 12(d))

Under the provisions of Section 12(d) the Attorney General can institute civil actions in Federal district courts to seek enforcement of the provisions of the Act described above—suspension of tests and devices, abolition of English literacy tests for citizens educated in foreign-language American schools, preclearance of election-law changes, and prohibition of discriminatory election laws.

[30]*City of Mobile v. Bolden*, 446 U.S. 55 (1980).

THE VOTING RIGHTS AMENDMENTS OF 1970 (P.L. 91-285)

Despite the registration of nearly one million new black voters, the litigation record following passage of the Act, a report of the Commission on Civil Rights, and testimony at congressional hearings soon revealed that various devices were being used to negate or diminish the newly gained voting strength of blacks.[31] They included:

1) Switching to at-large elections when black voting strength is concentrated in particular districts,
2) Extending the terms of incumbent white officials,
3) Making certain offices selective rather than elective,
4) Changing the dates of elections suddenly,
5) Changing the qualifications of candidates,
6) Increasing the costs of a filing fee for election, and
7) Gerrymandering to dilute the nonwhite vote.

After much debate, Congress amended the Voting Rights Act of 1965. The Voting Rights Amendments of 1970, signed into law on June 22, 1970, contained several new provisions that:

1) Extended the expiration date for five more years to August 1975,
2) Extended from five to 10 years the period of time for which an area covered by the Act must abstain from the use of any literacy test or similar device to discriminate against voters because of race or color,
3) Amended Section 4 of the Act to make the "trigger formula" cover three districts in Alaska; Apache County, Arizona; Imperial County, California; Elmore County, Idaho; Bronx, Kings (Brooklyn) and New York (Manhattan) counties, New York; and Wheeler County, Oregon
4) Suspended the use of literacy tests in all States until August 6, 1975,
5) Provided that any person could vote in a Presidential election if he had established residency 30 days prior to a Presidential election, and
6) Lowered the voting age to 18 years.[32]

---

[31]U.S. Commission on Civil Rights. *Political Participation*. Report, 1968. Washington, U.S. Govt. Print. Off., 1968. 256 p.

[32]P.L. 91-285, June 22, 1970; 84 Stat. 314; *Congressional Quarterly Almanac*, 91st Congress, 2nd Session...1970, Vol 26, Washington, D.C., Congressional Quarterly, Inc., 1971, p. 192-93.

Extension of Duration of the Act (Section 4(a))

Congress extended from five to ten years the period of time during which States and political subdivisions covered by the triggering provisions of Section 4(b) and seeking release from coverage must not have used any literacy test or device as a condition of voter registration with the purpose or effect of denying the right to vote on account of race.

Expansion of Coverage of the Act (Section 4(b)

In 1970, the amendments also changed the coverage formula of Section 4(b) to include any State or political subdivision that used a literacy test for voter registration on November 1, 1968, and in which less-than-50 percent registration or voting occurred in the 1968 presidential election. With the amendments, jurisdictions covered have to preclear election law changes made since November 1, 1968, and are subject to assignment of Federal examiners and election observers. The formula was extended from regional (Southern States) to national coverage. The extension was also intended to establish the principle that the effort to protect voting rights is not limited by a date in the past, i.e., 1964, but is ongoing.[33] Subdivisions in the following States were covered through the 1970 amendment of Section 4(b)—Arizona, California, Connecticut, Idaho, Massachusetts, New Hampshire, New York and Wyoming.

Ban on Literacy Tests

A new Section 201 imposed a ban on literacy tests and devices as conditions for voter registration in all jurisdictions in the country not already subject to the suspension of tests and devices under Section 4(a) until August 6, 1975. Thus, it was made coterminous with the suspension of literacy tests under Section 4(a). The rationale for this new provision was that the law should not discriminate against one part of the country, and that literacy requirements may prevent many minority citizens from voting in jurisdictions not covered by Section 4(a).[34]

---

[33] *Congressional Record*, v. 116, part 5, p. 6654-5.

[34] Ibid., v. 115, part 28, p. 38133-5; v. 116, part 4, p. 5521.

Residence Requirements (Section 202)

A new Section 202 provides that if a person applies for registration in his or her State not later than thirty days prior to the election, then he or she if otherwise qualified to vote, shall not be denied the right to vote in a Presidential election because of a residence requirement. If a citizen moved to another State after the thirtieth day preceding a Presidential election, that person has the right to vote in his or her former State.

Any citizen who is a resident of a State must be permitted to vote in a Presidential election by absentee ballot if he or she applies to that State not later than seven days prior to the election.

The Eighteen-Year-Old Vote (Section 302)

Section 302 of the Act grants the right to vote at age 18 in every primary and general election. Although the Supreme Court invalidated this provision for State and local elections, the 26th Amendment in 1971 guaranteed the right of eighteen-year-olds to vote in all elections.[35]

---

[35]*Oregon v. Mitchell*, 400 U.S. 112 (1970).

THE VOTING RIGHTS AMENDMENTS OF 1975 (P.L. 94-73)

In 1975, the Voting Rights Act came up for extension again. The Justice Department urged another five-year extension of the special coverage provisions of the Act, until 1980, in order to bring black political participation to levels comparable with that of whites, and to give an incentive to covered States to foster black registration and voting and, thereby, to demonstrate that special coverage is no longer needed.[36]

The Commission on Civil Rights recommended an additional ten-year extension of the Act, until 1985, for several reasons. Because black registration in the covered States was still below that of whites, and the proportion of black elected officials in covered States was low in comparison to the black percentage of the voting-age population in the covered States, there was a continuing need to foster black political participation. Another reason offered was that the Justice Department had only recently begun to enforce Section 5 (Federal preclearance of changes in election laws) effectively; therefore, enforcement of the preclearance requirement should continue. The Commission felt that Section 5 should remain in effect also to enable the Justice Department to monitor the electoral redistricting that would be required after the 1980 census. Such electoral redistricting would be required extensively under the "one man, one vote" rule, which mandates that electoral districts within States and political subdivisions be as nearly equal in population as possible. The Commission recommended extension of Section 5 so that this redistricting would be subject to Federal preclearance of election law changes in order to prevent dilution of black voting power through racial gerrymandering.

At congressional hearings, Congress heard Puerto Rican and Chicano voters and candidates for political office relate voting experiences that paralleled those of blacks. They pointed out that many Hispanics have difficulty filling out registration forms and understanding referenda and proposed constitutional amendments. They complained of inadequate or nonexistent bilingual election material; threats of economic reprisals for voting, location of polling places in areas where Chicanos were not welcomed, and burdensome absentee ballot procedures that resulted in limited numbers of migrant workers' voting. In addition, they accused the "Anglo" majority of reducing Hispanics to a minority

---

[36]U.S. Congress. House. Committee on the Judiciary. Subcommittee on Civil and Constitutional Rights. Extension of the Voting Rights Act. Hearings on H.R. 939 [and other bills]. 94th Congress, 1st session. Washington, U.S. Govt. Print. Off., 1975. p. 173-4 (testimony of Assistant Attorney General Pottinger).

of voters in previously Spanish-majority areas through annexations, gerrymandering of electoral districts, and at-large elections.[37]

After debate, Congress extended the Act for seven years, through August 6, 1982. The trigger formula provisions were continued for seven years, as well as the method by which jurisdictions could remove themselves from coverage; and it made permanent the temporary nationwide ban on use of literacy tests or similar devices. It extended coverage to more jurisdictions to protect the voting rights of ethnic groups whose language is other than English. The Voting Rights Amendments of 1975 were signed into law on August 6, 1975.[38]

Extension of Duration of Act (Section 4(a))

The 1975 amendments extended the duration of the temporary provisions of the Act for jurisdictions already covered an additional seven years, thus lengthening the period of coverage of these jurisdictions from ten to seventeen years. To accomplish this, Section 4(a) was amended to provide that any jurisdiction covered by Section 4(b) (the triggering formula) through determinations made with respect to the Presidential elections of 1964 or 1968 must not have used a discriminatory test or device for voter registration during the previous seventeen years in order to be released from coverage. Extension of coverage meant that jurisdictions originally covered in 1965 could not seek release from provisions of the Act until 1982, and those covered in 1970 until 1987. A seven-year instead of a five-year extension was enacted to ensure that jurisdictions covered in 1965 would not be released until two years after the 1980 census and to ensure that electoral redistricting as a result of the census would be subject to Federal preclearance under Section 5.[39]

Nationwide Ban on Literacy Tests (Section 201)

In 1975, Congress amended Section 201 to make permanent the prohibition of literacy tests for voter registration in noncovered jurisdictions and to extend it to jurisdictions already subject to the suspension of tests and devices under Section 4(a). This means that no covered jurisdiction could reinstitute tests or devices after release from coverage.

Extension of Coverage to Protect Language Minorities (Section 4(b))

Major provisions of the amended Voting Rights Act pertained to certain language minorities, defined in Section 14(c)(3) as persons of Spanish heritage,

---

[37]House Subcommittee on Civil and Constitutional Rights. Extension of the Voting Rights Act, p. 27-29, p. 519-35, 598-604, 800-28, 853-86, 922-32.

[38]P.L. 94-73, August 6, 1975; 89 Stat. 400.

[39]*Congressional Record*, v. 121, part 19, p. 24241-6.

American Indians, Asian Americans and Alaskan Natives. Preclearance and Federal observer protections were applied in any jurisdiction where:

1) The Census Bureau determined that more than 5 percent of the voting age citizens were of a single language minority;
2) Election materials had been printed only in English for the November 1, 1972, elections; and
3) Less than 50 percent of the voting age citizens had registered for or voted in the 1972 presidential election.

The presumption behind the new coverage formula was that in jurisdictions using literacy tests as conditions for voter registration, low rates of registration and voting result, in part at least, from discriminatory application of such tests. With respect to language minorities, English-only elections were presumed *ipso facto* to be discriminatory. The extension of Section 4(b) to protect language minorities covers the States of Alaska, Arizona and Texas and political subdivisions in California, Colorado, Florida, Hawaii, Michigan, New York, North Carolina and South Carolina.[40]

Jurisdictions Covered With Respect to Language Minorities Subject to Special Provisions of the Act (Sections 4(a), 5, 6, and 8)

Jurisdictions covered in 1975 with respect to language minorities are subject to the same provisions as are jurisdictions covered in 1965 and 1970. Under Section 4(a), jurisdictions covered in 1975 may not use any test or device as a condition for voter registration. Suspension of literacy tests for these jurisdictions means providing election materials in the language of the applicable language minority.[41] Such jurisdictions must preclear election-law changes enacted since November 1, 1972, pursuant to section 5, and are subject to assignment of examiners under Section 6 and of election observers under Section 8.

Duration of Coverage (Section 4(a))

Under Section 4(a) as amended in 1975, jurisdictions covered in that year with respect to language minorities were subject to the provisions of the Act for ten years instead of seventeen years, i.e., until 1985. They could be released from coverage by obtaining a declaratory judgment from the Federal District Court in the District of Columbia that the jurisdiction's English-only elections had not been a voting barrier during the last ten years.

---

[40]*Congressional Quarterly Almanac*, 94th Congress, 1st Session...1975, Vol 31, Washington, D.C., Congressional Quarterly, Inc., 1976, p. 521-23.

[41]Section 4(f)(4).

Bilingual-Election Requirement (Section 203)

Congress, with the addition of Section 203 in 1975, sought to increase the voter turnout of language minorities by requiring bilingual elections through August 6, 1985, if:

1) The Census Bureau determined that 5 percent of the jurisdiction's voting age citizens were of a single language minority, and
2) The illiteracy rate in English of the language minority was greater than the national English illiteracy rate. Illiteracy was defined as failure to complete 5th grade.

This section does not apply to any political subdivision in which each language minority is less than five percent even though any language minority resident in the political subdivision comprises more than five percent of the statewide population of voting age citizens. Jurisdictions covered by Section 203 are required to provide election materials and oral assistance in the language of the applicable language minority as well as in English. But jurisdictions that are covered only under Section 203 and not through the coverage formula of Section 4(b) are not subject to the other special provisions of the Act—preclearance of election laws, Federal examiners or Federal election observers.

A jurisdiction can be removed from this bilingual election requirement when it can demonstrate in Federal district court that the illiteracy rate of the language minority had dropped below the national illiteracy rate.

These bilingual requirements were scheduled to remain in effect for ten years, until 1985, the same duration as that of Section 4(b) coverage for language minorities. Subdivisions in the following States were covered by the bilingual election requirements of Section 203 (with considerable overlap of coverage under Sections 4(b) and 203): Alaska, Arizona, California, Colorado, Connecticut, Florida, Hawaii, Idaho, Kansas, Louisiana, Maine, Michigan, Minnesota, Mississippi, Montana, Nebraska, Nevada, New Mexico, New York, North Carolina, North Dakota, Oklahoma, Oregon, South Dakota, Texas, Utah, Virginia, Washington, Wisconsin and Wyoming.

Addition of Language-Minority Status to Section 2

As originally enacted, Section 2 forbade any jurisdiction in the country to enact an election law that denies or abridges voting rights on account of race or color. The 1975 amendments added language minorities to this section as a protected class.

Compilation of Registration and Voting Statistics (Section 207)

A new Section 207 requires the Census Bureau to compile registration and voting statistics in every jurisdiction covered by Section 4(a) for every statewide general election for United States Representatives after January 1, 1974, and in any jurisdiction for any election designated by the Civil Rights Commission. Census Bureau surveys are to include only a count of citizens of voting age, and of these by race or color and national origin, and determination of the extent to which such persons registered and voted. Section 207 provides that in making such surveys no participant shall be required to disclose his or her race, color, national origin, political party affiliation, or how he or she voted.

THE VOTING RIGHTS AMENDMENTS OF 1982 (P.L. 97-205)

Congress in 1982 amended Section 4(a) of the Voting Rights Act to enable jurisdictions to seek release from coverage in 1984 instead of their having to wait an additional five or more years as with previous amendments to the Act, provided they had not used a discriminatory test or device during a certain time period. Congress also amended Section 2 to provide that courts could judge an election law to be discriminatory without proof that it was *intended* to be so, but if it *results* in abridging minority voting power.

On August 6, 1982, jurisdictions originally covered by the Act in 1965 could have sought release from its provisions by showing in the U.S. District Court for the District of Columbia that they had not used a discriminatory literacy test or device as a condition for voter registration during the previous seventeen years. Instead of allowing this termination of coverage to occur, Congress amended the Act in 1982 to prevent immediate release of these jurisdictions in order to protect "the ability of minorities to participate effectively within the political process."[42] The House Judiciary Committee noted that blacks and other minorities may not yet be "in a position to compete in the political arena against non-minorities on an equal basis,"[43] and that, despite increased registration and voting and election of blacks to public office, they still may be vulnerable "to attempts by opponents of equality to diminish their political influence."[44]

At the same time, it was perceived that covered jurisdictions would be given little incentive to foster minority political participation if they could not obtain release from coverage until the expiration of a certain number of years, regardless of their efforts to encourage such participation. The 1982 amendments were intended to provide such incentive by offering the possibility of release in the near future to States and political subdivisions that tried to promote minority political participation. The 1982 amendments to the Act sought to accomplish these objectives by allowing jurisdictions to seek release from coverage after only two more years, instead of five or more as heretofore, but by permitting them to be released only after meeting other conditions than the former requirement of not having used a discriminatory test or device for voter registration.

The amended Voting Rights Act of 1982 has four major provisions. It

1) Extends the preclearance section of the Act for 25 years,
2) Requires 9 States and portions of 13 others to obtain preclearance

---

[42]U.S. Congress. House. Committee on the Judiciary. Voting Rights Act Extension. Report to accompany H.R. 3112. 97th Congress, 1st session, H. Rept. No. 97-227. Washington, U.S. Govt. Print. Off., 1981. p. 11.

[43]Ibid.

[44]Ibid.

from the Justice Department before making any changes in election laws or procedures,

3) Substitutes new language that overturned a 1980 Supreme Court ruling in the case of *Mobile v. Bolden* that an intent to discriminate must be shown to prove a violation and allowed certain voting rights violations under Section 2 to be proved by showing that an election law or procedure had resulted in discrimination,
4) Extends provisions requiring certain areas of the country to provide bilingual election materials until 1992. (The old expiration date was 1985.)

The Voting Rights Act Amendments of 1982 were signed into law on June 29, 1982.[45]

Extension of Duration of the Act (Section 4(a))

The 1982 amendments extended the current provisions of the Act for two years, which meant that the period of time during which States and political subdivisions seeking release under Section 4(a) could not have used a discriminatory test or device as a condition for voter registration was increased from seventeen to nineteen years. (The ten-year period for jurisdictions covered in 1975 with respect to language minorities was not changed.) Congress decided to hold jurisdictions that were covered in 1965 under the Act for two more years, from 1982 until 1984, for two reasons. The first reason was to give the Justice Department time to prepare for the large number of court actions for release that were expected as soon as the conditions for release were changed.[46]

The second reason was to ensure that redistricting in covered jurisdictions necessitated by the 1980 census (which had not been completed by 1982) would still be covered by the Section 5 preclearance requirement. It will be recalled that the Congress, in 1975, extended that Act for seven years, until two years after the 1980 census, so that covered jurisdictions would have to submit their new electoral districts for Federal preclearance. This preclearance enabled the Justice Department and the U.S. District Court for the District of Columbia to guarantee that such redistricting would not abridge or dilute black or Hispanic voting power. Congressional redistricting had to be completed before the 1982 elections. But there were other—State and local—elections for which redistricting might not have to have been completed until after 1982, and

---

[45]P.L. 97-205; 96 Stat. 131; *Congressional Quarterly Almanac*, 97th Congress, 2nd Session...1982, Vol 38, Washington, D.C., Congressional Quarterly, Inc., 1983, p. 373-74.

[46]House Committee on the Judiciary. Voting Rights Act Extension. H. Rept. 97-227, p. 39.

Congress extended the current provisions of the Act from 1982 until 1984 so that such redistricting would also be reviewed at the Federal level.[47]

Amended Conditions for Release from Coverage (Section 4(a))

The 1982 amendments provide that on August 5, 1984, any jurisdiction covered in 1965, 1970 or 1975 may be released from coverage if it can show in the U.S. District Court for the District of Columbia that it has met the following conditions during the preceding ten years:

1) It has not used a discriminatory test or device for voter registration;
2) No court has found it to have denied or abridged voting rights;
3) It had complied with the preclearance requirement of Section 5 by submitting all election-law changes for Federal review;
4) There has been no Federal objection to any election law change submitted under Section 5;
5) No Federal examiners have been assigned to the jurisdiction;
6) It has fostered political participation by minority citizens; and
7) It can present evidence of minority registration, voting and other political participation.

The U.S. District Court for the District of Columbia is to retain jurisdiction of any action for release from coverage for ten years, and is to reopen the case if the Attorney General or an aggrieved person alleges that voting discrimination has occurred. No jurisdiction may be released from coverage while it is defending itself in a voting rights case, provided that the case was initiated prior to the jurisdiction's filing a court action for release from coverage. This proviso was added to prevent persons or groups from precluding a jurisdiction from seeking release simply by filing a voting rights suit in court.[48]

Separate Release for Political Subdivisions (Section 4(a))

Prior to the 1982 amendments, only a State covered statewide or a political subdivision of a noncovered State could seek release from coverage. Congress amended Section 4(a) in 1982 to allow a political subdivision of a covered State to obtain release from coverage separately.

Reconsideration and Termination of the Act (Section 4(a))

The 1982 amendments provide that Congress shall "reconsider" the special, administrative provisions of the Act (preclearance of election-law changes and assignment of examiners and election observers) 15 years after the effective date

---

[47] *Congressional Record* (daily ed.), v. 127, p. H6974.

[48] For a further discussion of Section 4 see the following report: U.S. Library of Congress. Congressional Research Service. The Voting Rights Act of 1965: A Legal Overview. Report by L. Paige Whitaker. Washington, 1991, p. 10-13.

of the 1982 amendments, in 1997; and that these provisions shall expire 25 years after this effective date, in 2007.

Extension of Bilingual-Election Requirement (Section 203)

The 1982 amendments extended the bilingual election provisions of Section 203 for seven years, until August 6, 1992. Amendments further provide that the count of members of any language minority in a jurisdiction is to be limited to those who cannot read English well enough to use English-language registration and voting materials, as determined by the Census Bureau in the 1980 census and in studies conducted thereafter. This limitation on the counting of language-minority members applies only to Section 203. In counting members of a language minority to determine whether a jurisdiction is covered under Section 4(b), all members are counted even if they can read English well enough to register and vote in English.

Following enactment of the 1982 amendment to Section 203, the Census Bureau determined that one or more political subdivisions in the following twenty States were subject to the bilingual election requirement: Alaska, Arizona, California, Colorado, Connecticut, Florida, Hawaii, Idaho, Massachusetts, Michigan, Montana, New Jersey, New Mexico, New York, North Dakota, Oklahoma, South Dakota, Texas, Utah, and Wisconsin.[49]

Amendment to Judicial Standard of Proof Under Section 2

In the 1980 case of *City of Mobile v. Bolden*,[50] the Supreme Court affirmed that the proper standard for courts to use in deciding cases under Section 2 was demonstration of discriminatory intention. The Court said that courts can find any law to be in violation of the Fourteenth or Fifteenth Amendment only if it is shown that the law was enacted with the *purpose* or *intention* of discriminating. Because it regarded Section 2 of the Voting Rights Act as a statutory restatement of the Fifteenth Amendment, the Court held that the same judicial standard—intent—applies to cases brought under Section 2. [51]

To make it easier to challenge discriminatory election laws, Congress amended Section 2 to establish discriminatory *effect* or *result* as a standard of proof in voting rights cases. Amendments made it easier to prove in court that a jurisdiction enacted a law that denies or abridges the right to vote on account of race or language-minority status in violation of Section 2. For example, if elections for the city council in a majority-white city were conducted at-large,

---

[49]49 *Federal Register* 25887, June 25, 1984. This list replaced the list of covered jurisdictions published after the 1975 amendments to the Act (see page 19).

[50]446 U.S. 55.

[51]Ibid., at 60-1.

with the result that black voters were unable to elect even one councilman of their own choice, blacks, prior to 1982, could have prevailed in a court suit seeking an injunction against the at-large election law only if they could have proven that it was instituted for the deliberate purpose of preventing black candidates from being elected. Discriminatory motivation is often difficult to prove. After the 1982 amendment to Section 2, they might obtain such an injunction by pointing out that blacks are unable to elect any of their own candidates, because of the discriminatory result of the at-large system.

Congress recognized the danger in adopting a "results" standard for Section 2, namely, that electoral outcomes in which black voters fail to elect their own candidates in numbers proportional to the percentage that blacks comprise of the total electorate might be adduced as evidence sufficient to eliminate any at-large electoral systems through court suits. In this way, the results standard could have led to acceptance of a right of racial- or ethnic-group proportional representation. To avoid this conclusion, Congress provided that racially or ethnically unequal results of an electoral system may indicate a violation of Section 2 only if such results occur within a wider context of discrimination against a racial or ethnic minority. Where such official or societal discrimination is absent, unequal results of an electoral system would not alone result in a violation of Section 2.

The 1982 amendments of Section 2 forbid application of any law "in a manner which results in a denial or abridgment" of the voting rights of members of protected classes—blacks and members of language minorities. Section 2 now provides that a court may find such a violation of voting rights if, within a community characterized by widespread discrimination, it determines that either of the following conditions obtains:

1) party nominating procedures deny equal opportunity for members of protected classes to have persons of their own choice selected as candidates for election to public office; or
2) the method of election denies equal opportunity for members of protected classes to elect candidates of their own choice to public office.

Section 2 states that "the extent to which members of a protected class have been elected to office" in the jurisdiction is one factor that may be considered in the totality of circumstances, but it provides that a protected class has no right to have its members elected to office in numbers proportional to their percentage in the population.

To prove a violation of Section 2, it must be shown that either of the above conditions occurs as part of a "totality of circumstances" constituting societal discrimination and racial or ethnic polarization, as evidenced, for example, by: a history of official discrimination, residual effects of discrimination in education, employment and health; expressed racism in election campaigns; unresponsiveness of elected officials to needs of the minority community; and racial bloc voting if it is indicative of racial antagonism.[52]

The new standard of proof under Section 2 is not, then, a pure "results" standard that might open the way to challenges of electoral systems throughout the country in which minorities cannot achieve proportional representation. Rather, it is a standard by which electoral results may be adduced as evidence of discrimination if an apparently fair electoral system—i.e., one that meets the "one man, one vote" principle—in fact serves to perpetuate the domination of a white "power structure" to the disadvantage of a minority group.

---

[52]U.S. Congress. Senate. Committee on the Judiciary. Voting Rights Act Extension. Report on S. 1992. 97th Congress, 2d session, S. Rept. No. 97-417. Washington, U.S. Govt. Print. Off., 1982. p. 28-30.

SUMMARY OF CURRENT MAJOR PROVISIONS OF THE ACT

Following is a summary of the major provisions of the Voting Rights Act in effect at the present time.[53]

Coverage (Section 4(b))

A State or political subdivision of a State is subject to the administrative enforcement provisions of the Act if it maintained a literacy test or device (such as the requirement that a qualified voter vouch for the eligibility of a registration applicant) as a condition for voter registration on November 1, of 1964, 1968 or 1972, and either less than 50 percent of age-eligible citizens were registered to vote or less than 50 percent of such citizens voted in the presidential election held in the year in which it used such a test or device. Use of a literacy test on November 1, 1972, means that a jurisdiction in which more than five percent of the voting-age population is of a single language minority (American Indian, Alaskan Native, Asian American or of Spanish heritage) conducted elections with exclusively English-language materials or assistance.[54]

Suspension of Tests and Devices (Section 4(a))

Jurisdictions covered under the Act through one of the coverage formulas of Section 4(b) may not use any test or device as a condition of voter registration. With respect to jurisdictions covered through 1972 criteria, suspension of tests and devices means providing electoral materials and assistance in the language of the applicable language minority as well as in English.

Preclearance of Election-Law Changes (Section 5)

Covered jurisdictions are required to submit for Federal review any change in law affecting elections before putting such a law into effect. As jurisdictions have been covered because they used literacy tests for voter registration and had

---

[53]For a detailed discussion of the Voting Rights Act of 1965, as amended, see the following reports: U.S. Library of Congress. Congressional Research Service. The Voting Rights Act of 1965: A Legal Overview. Report, by L. Paige Whitaker. Washington, 1991; U.S. Library of Congress. Congressional Research Service. Congressional and State Reapportionment and Redistricting: A Legal Analysis. Report, by Thomas M. Durbin and L. Paige Whitaker. Washington, 1991.

[54]Jurisdictions covered under Section 4(b) are listed in 28 C.F.R. 51.54, Appendix. Those covered for language minorities are also listed in 28 C.F.R. 55.24, Appendix. This Appendix indicates the minority language applicable for each jurisdiction.

low political participation in the 1964, 1968 or 1972 presidential election, they must submit election-law changes made since November 1 of 1964, 1968 or 1972, respectively. They must submit such changes in law either to the U.S. Justice Department or the U.S. District Court for the District of Columbia to ensure that new laws affecting elections do not have the purpose and will not have the effect of denying or abridging voting rights on account of race, color or language-minority status. The jurisdiction may put a new law into effect if it has submitted it to the Attorney General and the latter has not objected to it within 60 days.

Federal Examiners to List Eligible Voters (Section 6)

At the request of the Justice Department, the U.S. Office of Personnel Management is to send one or more Federal examiners to list eligible voters for registration in a covered political subdivision of a State whenever the Department receives 20 or more written complaints of voting discrimination on account of race, color or language-minority status, or whenever the Attorney General thinks it is necessary to protect voting rights.

Federal Election Observers (Section 8)

The Attorney General may request the Office of Personnel Management to send Federal observers to any jurisdiction where an examiner has been assigned. Observers are to ensure that all registered voters are allowed to vote, and that all votes are properly counted.

Conditions for Release From Coverage (Section 4(a))

A covered State or political subdivision of a State, whether the subdivision was covered as part of a covered State or separately, may be released from required preclearance of election law changes under Section 5 and from being subject to assignment both of examiners under Section 6 and of observers under Section 8 if it can meet several specified conditions. It must be able to demonstrate in an action for a declaratory judgment in the U.S. District Court for the District of Columbia that during the previous ten years:

1) It has not used a discriminatory test or device for voter registration;
2) It has not been found in a court case to have denied or abridged voting rights, and it has not agreed through a consent decree to discontinue any discriminatory practice with respect to voting;
3) It has precleared all election-law changes with the Justice Department or with the U.S. District Court for the District of Columbia;
4) It has not received a single objection to an election-law change submitted for Federal preclearance;
5) No Federal examiner has been assigned to the jurisdiction;
6) It has promoted political participation by racial or language minorities; and

7) It can present evidence of minority registration, voting and other political participation.

The U.S. District Court for the District of Columbia is to retain jurisdiction over any action for release from coverage for ten years, and is to reopen the case whenever during that time period either the Attorney General or an aggrieved person alleges that voting discrimination has occurred in the jurisdiction.

A jurisdiction cannot be released from coverage while it is defending itself in a voting rights case, unless the case was filed in court after the jurisdiction initiated a court action for release from coverage.

Termination of Coverage Provisions (Section 4(a))

Congress shall reconsider provisions that require preclearance of election-law changes and assignments of examiners and election observers in 1997. These provisions are due to expire in 2007.

Prohibitions of English-Language Literacy Requirement for Citizens Educated in American Schools (Section 4(e))

Any citizen educated in an American-flag school in which classroom instruction is given in a language other than English (e.g., a public school in Puerto Rico in which instruction is given in Spanish) may not be denied the right to vote because he or she cannot meet an English-language literacy requirement.

Bilingual-Election Requirement (Section 203)

A State or political subdivision in which the Census Bureau determines that more than five percent of the citizens of voting age are of a single language minority (American Indian, Alaskan Native, Asian American or of Spanish heritage) whose illiteracy rate (failure to complete the fifth grade) is higher than the national illiteracy rate must provide election materials and assistance in the language of the applicable minority as well as in English. Only members of a language minority who cannot read English well enough to use English-language election materials are counted.

If the language minority comprises less than five percent of the voting age population of a political subdivision, that subdivision is not covered by Section 203 even if the language minority comprises more than five percent of the Statewide population.

This bilingual election requirement is due to expire on August 6, 1992.[55]

---

[55]Jurisdictions covered under Section 203 are listed in 28 C.F.R. 55.24, Appendix. The listing indicates the applicable minority language for each jurisdiction.

Nationwide Literacy Test Ban (Section 201)

Every jurisdiction in the country is forbidden to impose a literacy test or device, such as a voucher requirement, as a condition for voter registration.

Registration and Voting Statistics (Section 207)

The Census Bureau is to compile statistics in every covered jurisdiction showing the extent to which all citizens of voting age and all such citizens by race, color and national origin registered and voted in every congressional election after January 1, 1974. It is also to compile these statistics in any jurisdiction and for any election designated by the U.S. Civil Rights Commission. No person whom the Census Bureau questions may be compelled to state his or her race, color, national origin, political party affiliation or how he or she voted.

Limitation of Residence Requirements for Voting (Section 202)

No State may deny any citizen the right to vote in a Presidential election if he or she registers to vote at least 30 days prior to the election. If a citizen moves to another State after the 30th day preceding a Presidential election, that person may vote in his or her former State.

If a citizen applies for an absentee ballot seven days before a Presidential election, then no State may deny him or her the right to vote in the election.

General Prohibition of Discriminatory Voting Laws (Section 2)

Section 2 prohibits any State or political subdivision of a State from putting into effect an election law (which results in a denial or abridgment) of voting rights on account of race, color or language-minority (American Indian, Alaskan Native, Asian American or of Spanish heritage) status.

A court may find a violation of Section 2 if a protected class is disadvantaged by official and social discrimination and either political nominating processes or a method of election denies to the protected class equal opportunity to elect to office candidates of its own choice. Section 2 does not grant to any protected class a right to elect a number of candidates to public office in proportion to the percentage that class comprises of the total electorate.

Civil Actions to Enforce Compliance (Section 12(d))

Section 12(d) authorizes the Attorney General to seek compliance enforcement through the Federal district courts.

IMPACT OF THE VOTING RIGHTS ACT OF 1965, AS AMENDED

Blacks

The Voting Rights Act of 1965 had considerable impact on the numbers of blacks registered to vote. Within four years of 1965, 800,000 applicants had registered to vote in areas where they were once denied the franchise by literacy tests and other devices. Blacks have made considerable progress not only in the numbers of black elected officials (from 1,469 in 1970 to 7,370 in 1990), but in the ranks of those elected. That is, blacks were elected to Congress, to statewide offices, and to county and municipal offices. In 1970, 10 blacks were elected to Congress; by 1990, 24 were elected to Congress. At the State level, 168 blacks served as legislators in 1970; in 1990, 415 served. The numbers of black elected officials at the county and municipal levels increased from 92 in 1970 to 3,671 in 1990.[56]

Hispanics

Evidence reveals that the addition of bilingual language provisions was effective in increasing Hispanic participation in the political process. Subsequent to the addition of the bilingual provisions of the Act, the number of Hispanics registered to vote in the Southwest doubled from 1976 to 1988 from 1,512,300 to 3,003,400. The number of elected Hispanic officials rose significantly as well—from 1,379 in 1973 to 4,202 in 1991. In 1991, eleven Hispanics served in Congress; 140 served at the State level; and 1,692 at the county and municipal levels.[57]

Asian Americans

Although the numbers of Asian Americans and Pacific Islanders have grown steadily to 7.274 million, they constitute only 2.9% of the total U.S. population. However, despite this growth rate there are few Asian American elected officials. The single largest factor that is often cited as preventing Asian Americans from registering and participating in the electoral process is the language barrier. Asian Americans comprise about ten percent of the population of the State of California; yet, there are only two Asian American congressmen, and, on the State level, only one elected position held by an Asian American—secretary of

---

[56]Joint Center for Political and Economic Studies, *Black Elected Officials, A National Roster, 1989*, Joint Center for Political Studies Press, Washington, D.C. 1989, p. 10; Joint Center for Political and Economic Studies, *Black Elected Officials, A National Roster, 1990*, Joint Center for Political and Economic Studies Press, Washington, D.C., p. 1-5.

[57]National Association of Latino Elected and Appointed Officials Educational Fund, *1990 National Roster of Hispanic Elected Officials*, 1991, The NALEO Educational Fund, Inc., Washington, D.C., p. vii-viii.

state. At the local level a similar picture surfaces. In Daly City, California, Asian Americans are 42 percent of the population, but no Asian American has been elected to the city council. The largest Asian American community in the Nation (with a population of about 600,000) is in New York City, yet no Asian American has been elected to either the city council, State assembly or State senate.[58]

Native Americans

Some Native Americans have benefitted from the bilingual assistance provisions of Section 203. The Navajo Nation reports that both the numbers of registered Navajo voters and the Navajo voter turnout has increased since 1976. This increase in voter registration and voter turnout has influenced the number of elected Navajos to county and State government. Since 1972, four senators and ten representatives have been elected to State legislatures in Arizona, New Mexico and Utah. In these same States eighteen county seats including county commissioners, county board of election supervisors and a sheriff have been filled by Navajos.[59]

---

[58]U.S. Congress. Senate. Committee on the Judiciary. Subcommittee on the Constitution. Hearings on the Voting Rights Act Language Assistance Amendments, 1992. February 26, 1992 (testimony of Charles Pei Wang, Vice Chair, U.S. Commission on Civil Rights).

[59]U.S. Congress. House. Committee on the Judiciary. Subcommittee on Civil and Constitutional Rights. Hearings on the Voting Rights Act Language Assistance Amendments, 1992. April 1, 1992 (testimony of Faith Roessel, Director of the Navajo Nation Washington Office).

COST OF BILINGUAL ELECTION ASSISTANCE

Section 203 of the Voting Rights Act requires covered States and political subdivisions to provide registration or voting materials or oral assistance in the language of the applicable minority if more than five percent of the citizens of voting age are of a single language minority (American Indian, Alaskan Native, Asian American, or Spanish heritage) and if the illiteracy rate (failure to complete the fifth grade) of such language minority is higher than the national illiteracy rate.

Cost of Language Assistance

Written. In 1986, the General Accounting Office (GAO) prepared a report on the costs and use of bilingual voting assistance during the November 6, 1984, general election that was based on data obtained through exit polls it sponsored in Texas, and responses from covered State governments. Of 295 jurisdictions that responded to the GAO questionnaire, an estimated 83 incurred $388,000 in additional costs to provide written assistance. This figure represents an average of about 7.6 percent of their total costs for the general election. GAO estimated that eighteen additional States provided written assistance but incurred no costs to do so.

Additional costs associated with the provision of minority language text in election publications result from translating text into the minority language, higher printing costs for using more paper and ink, and the extra time needed for typesetting and proofreading.[60]

Oral. Of 259 responding jurisdictions that reported providing oral assistance, GAO estimated no additional costs were incurred by 205. An estimated 15 of these jurisdictions did not know the amount of additional costs they incurred in providing bilingual assistance. The 39 jurisdictions that provided oral assistance spent about $30,000 for it. This figure represents an average of about 2.8 percent of their costs to hold the November 6, 1984, general election.

A majority of jurisdictions did not incur costs for providing oral assistance for several reasons. Some did not hire additional workers; rather, they found poll workers who were able to converse in the covered minority language. Usually, jurisdictions paid bilingual and monolingual poll workers at the same rate. In other cases, rather than hiring a bilingual worker for polling places, they made someone available if the polling place indicated a need for language

---

[60]United States General Accounting Office, Bilingual Voting Assistance, Costs of and Use During the November 1984 General Election; Report to the Congress by the Comptroller General of the United States. GGD-86-134BR, September 1986, Washington, 1986. p. 16-17.

assistance. Even then, standby workers were often unpaid volunteers or were paid only if they actually provided oral assistance at the polling place.[61]

Use of Language Assistance

Eighty percent of 277 jurisdictions that had provided written assistance on official ballots could not estimate the number of people who used the assistance. Jurisdictions lacked this information because they overwhelmingly used a bilingual format for election materials with both English and the minority language in one document, and also used voting machines to accommodate the bilingual needs of voters.

Of the 49 officials who could estimate the use of minority language assistance available on official ballots in their jurisdictions, 26 said that no one used the assistance. Twenty-three officials using professional judgment, requests for ballots, minority language statistics, and other bases, singularly or in combination, estimated that from 1 to 7,500 people used the assistance on official ballots. Based on exit poll interviews with voters, GAO estimated that 69,000 of approximately 275,000 Hispanics who voted in the 1,012 Texas precincts used written assistance on election day.[62]

Seventy-four percent of responding jurisdictions that provided oral assistance were unable to estimate the number of voters who received the assistance. Of the 62 jurisdictions that offered estimates of oral assistance, 29 reported that no one used the assistance and 33 provided estimates ranging from one to 2,634 people. About 85,000 out of 263,000 Hispanic voters received oral assistance in Spanish.[63]

---

[61]Ibid., p. 19-20.

[62]Ibid., p. 26.

[63]Ibid., p. 32-34.

ISBN 1-56072-173-1

RACE ISSUES IN THE UNITED STATES BASED ON NATIONAL PUBLIC OPINION POLLS*

M.A. Aubin

SUMMARY

This report presents national public opinion polls on race issues in the United States, conducted between January 1988 and March 1992. It is another in a series of poll compilations by CRS on selected major policy issues.

Several findings are worth noting. There is evidence that a majority of blacks and whites do not feel uncomfortable with interracial contact. An April 1991 Newsweek Poll found that only 6 percent of the white respondents and 17 percent of the black respondents said they were "uncomfortable working with members of another race." Blacks and whites differ, however, in their views on the status of race relations. A March 1992 Washington Post Poll found that 34 percent of whites felt that race relations were "excellent" or "good" and 64 percent felt race relations were "not-so-good" or "poor" while responses for blacks were 21 percent and 78 percent respectively.

* Excerpted from CIS Report 92-428.

Despite some feelings of progress in the area of civil rights, Americans believe that discrimination continues to exist—the March 1992 Washington Post Poll found that only 10 percent of whites and 9 percent of blacks felt that "discrimination against blacks is no longer a problem in the United States." The way the questions were worded had an effect on how the public felt about policies that are designed to correct discrimination. When presented with a question as to whether they favored preferential treatment as a policy to help minorities in employment and education, the public responded negatively. However, when "affirmative action" was mentioned as a policy proposal, the public responded more favorably. Despite this difference in opinion concerning policy, a large majority of the public agreed on what *specific* programs they would like to see implemented for minorities. An example of this consensus appears in a June 1991 Gallup Poll: 73 percent favored "spending more money to improve schools in black communities," 83 percent favored "more Head Start programs to provide preschool education" and 72 percent favored "spending more federal funds on job training programs" for blacks.

Blacks and whites were divided on what actions the Federal government should take to correct discrimination and help minorities. A May 1991 NBC News/Wall Street Journal poll showed that 82 percent of the black respondents felt that the "federal government should make special efforts to improve the position of blacks and other minority groups to correct past discrimination" while 39 percent of the whites held this view. According to these polls, blacks and whites were also split on the effectiveness of current civil rights laws. A June 1991 NBC News/Wall Street Journal poll showed that 60 percent of blacks and 18 percent of whites thought that "current laws need to be toughened," 10 percent of blacks and 26 percent of whites thought that "current laws are right, and protect minorities well enough" and 24 percent of blacks and 50 percent of whites said that "current laws have gone too far."

PREFACE

THE ROLE OF PUBLIC OPINION POLLS

Public opinion polls appear to be capturing more and more of the public's attention. As it is, we are inundated with the seemingly constant release of opinion polls on almost every subject. Along with the increased prominence of polls, debate over their influence on the political process has intensified.[1] Some argue that poll results unduly influence elections and the direction of public policy. Others maintain that even if the polls themselves do not measurably alter public opinion, public officials behave as if they did. Furthermore some experts argue that no measurable effects of polls on opinion formation have been proven. However, while the effect of opinion poll results on the political process is debatable, they undoubtedly do have an impact on what the press writes about and how much emphasis it gives to a story and, in the case of election contests, they can affect such things as a candidate's ability to attract campaign contributions and choice of political advisors.

While it is not the purpose of this report to take a position in this debate, the fact remains that although public opinion poll results are sometimes promoted as precise measurements, they are really illusions of precision. Poll results may be misleading or interpreted poorly or inaccurately. On the other hand, polls may provide valuable information on what the public thinks; as such they can enhance the political process. This report and the series of which it is a part are intended to facilitate the latter process.

An informative poll can provide not only the prevalence and direction of opinion but also the intensity with which individuals hold a particular viewpoint. A. Lawrence Lowell, one of the fathers of public opinion research, argued that if one wants to predict public behavior regarding a particular policy issue, then unanimity is not necessary and a majority is not enough. What counts instead is the intensity with which the opinions are held.[2] This view holds that intensity is more likely to predict behavior than direction alone.

---

[1] Generally, public opinion polls are used to see how different publics view various issues and to predict election races.

[2] Lowell, A. Lawrence. *Public Opinion and Popular Government*. New York, Johnson Reprint Corporation, 1969. p. 1-15; Martin, John L. *The Genealogy of Public Opinion Polling in Polling and the Democratic Consensus*. Beverly Hills, California, Sage Publications, 1984. p. 15.

Opinion can be different depending on whether people have strong convictions or weak convictions or whether they are highly informed or not well informed.[3]

One of the best standards by which to interpret the validity of a finding is to compare results to the same question over time. This is difficult at times because pollsters tend to ask questions on issues that are of current interest and worded accordingly. However, comparing responses to similar questions with only slightly different wording can help determine whether opinion on the issue is malleable or not. Also, comparing the responses for one question with those for slightly different but related issues gives us an ability to better distinguish the kinds of policies the public may be willing to support.[4] For example, explanations of the public view on National Health Care would be facilitated by polls that asked whether or not the public supported such a policy, how strong that support or opposition was, whether they would be willing to pay additional taxes for such a policy and if so, how much.

Finally, it is important to bear in mind that a definitive statement on how the public feels on most public policy issues is impossible. Most public issues do not embody a singular concept; each issue brings with it multiple concerns--legal, moral, ethical, social, political, economic, and technical.[5] Guidelines for interpreting public opinion polls can be found in the appendix.

CRS'S POLLS DATABASE FILE

Many of the poll results contained in this report have been drawn from the Congressional Research Service's on-line POLLS (Public Opinion Legislative Locator Service) database file located on the Library of Congress' SCORPIO system. The POLLS file contains the results of public opinion surveys, as reported in news releases or printed studies, conducted by some of the major public opinion polling organizations. The POLLS file was originally developed for CRS by the Survey Research Center at the University of California, Berkeley.

The POLLS file contains the reported results of: the Harris Survey, the Gallup Poll, the CBS News/New York Times Poll, and the NBC News Poll (NBC News/Wall Street Journal, as of October 1985), all since January 1, 1978. The POLLS file also contains the results of the Los Angeles Times Poll since January 1982 and the ABC News/Washington Post Poll since January 1985.

---

[3] Erikson, Robert S., Norman R. Luttbeg and Kent L. Tedin. *American Public Opinion: Its Origins, Content, and Impact*. 3rd ed., New York, Macmillan Publishing Company, 1988. p. 50.

[4] Ibid., p. 55-56.

[5] Childs, Harwood L. *Introduction*. In: Lowell, Lawrence A. *Public Opinion and Popular Government*. New York, Johnson Reprint Corporation, 1969. p. xi.

Information from these sources is added to the file continually. The POLLS file also contains the results of selected special surveys conducted for government agencies and private organizations. We are also indebted to the Roper Center for obtaining and converting numerous polls for the POLLS file. As new studies of likely interest to Members of Congress are released, they are added to the database.

The CRS Government Division also maintains an extensive hardcopy file of public opinion polls from many polling organizations covering a wide array of subjects. Materials from these files are used in this report to supplement data from the POLLS file.

Limitations of the POLLS File and the Hardcopy File

The accuracy of the information contained in the POLLS file and the hardcopy file is dependent on the accuracy of the published source from which the information is taken. While CRS makes every effort to check the POLLS file database information against the original published version, it is not routinely possible, for either the POLLS file or the hardcopy file, to verify the original published version against the actual data collected or to verify the description of the actual field procedures used by the various organizations.

Even though both files provide results from various polling organizations, they do not include *all* the public opinion results on any topic. Furthermore, the results shown in both files are limited by what the polling organizations send to CRS.

For More Information On Using The POLLS Database File

If you require a more detailed search on a particular topic beyond what is contained in this publication, you can request further research from CRS or, through SCORPIO, directly access the POLLS file in your congressional office. For information and training on using the POLL file directly from the terminals in your office, contact Ted Moore at 707-6447. For information about specific polls call 707-8646. This service is limited to congressional users only.

I. DEMOGRAPHICS AND PUBLIC OPINION ON RACE ISSUES

The racial and ethnic composition of America has changed over the past decade. Table 1 displays the results of the Census Bureau's data on population distribution in the United States by race and Hispanic origin for 1980 and 1990. Between 1980 and 1990, the minority population has grown as a percentage of the general population. Concerning minority racial composition, the Asian and Pacific Islander subgroup has grown the most *percentage*-wise (107.8 percent). In actual *numbers*, the black population has grown the most — from 26,495,025 in 1980 to 29,986,060 in 1990 for an increase of 3,491,035 people. Other increases in the minority population from 1980 to 1990 are: American Indian, Eskimo or Aleut: 538,834; Asian and Pacific Islander: 3,773,223; and other races: 3,046,528.

Those of Hispanic origin grew from 6.4 percent of the general population in 1980 to 9 percent in 1990 for an increase of 53 percent. The Hispanic population as a whole went from 14,608,673 in 1980 to 22,354,059 in 1990 for a change of 7,745,386.

The white population as a *percentage of the overall population* in the United States dipped from 83.1 percent to 80.3 percent for a change of 6 percent. From 1980 to 1990 the *number* of whites in the United States increased from 188,371,622 to 199,686,070 for an increase of 11,314,448.

TABLE 1. Population Distribution by Race and Hispanic Origin

	1980 Census	1990 Census	Percent Change
Race			
White	83.1 %	80.3 %	-6.0 %
Black	11.7	12.1	13.2
American Indian, Eskimo, Aleut	0.6	0.8	37.9
Asian, Pacific Islander	1.5	2.9	107.8
Other race	3.0	3.9	45.1
Hispanic Origin			
Hispanic origin	6.4	9.0	53.0
Not of Hispanic origin	93.6	91.0	-6.8

United States Department of Commerce News, Economics and Statistics Administration, Bureau of the Census. [June 12, 1991, CB91-215].

The public's perception of the racial and ethnic composition of the United States differs from the actual numbers cited in the census. A March 1990 Gallup Poll asked the general public to guess the percentage of the population that they thought was black (see Table 2); 87 percent responded with estimates of over 15 percent. These estimates were high compared to the actual 1990 proportion of 12.1 percent. Estimates by the public of the proportion Hispanic people in the general population were also above that of actual numbers in the 1990 census (69 percent responded with estimates of over 10 percent while the actual proportion is 9.0 percent). Data on the public's perception of the racial composition of the United States with respect to other minority groups was not available.

TABLE 2. Percentage of Black and Hispanic Population in the U.S.?

March 1990

"What percent of the U.S. population today would you say is black?"

Less than 10 percent	2 %
Between 10 and 14	8
Between 15 and 19	7
Between 20 and 29	21
Between 30 and 39	22
Between 40 and 49	16
50 percent or more	13
Don't know	11

"What percent of the U.S. population today would you say is Hispanic?"

Less than 5 percent	3 %
Between 5 and 9	12
Between 10 and 19	28
Between 20 and 29	20
Between 30 and 49	16
50 percent or more	5
Don't know	16

The Gallup Poll. (The results of the survey are based on telephone interviews with a national sample of 1,225 adults, aged 18 and over, contacted during the period March 15-18, 1990.)

Public opinion polls also indicate concentrations of individual race groups in neighborhoods. A January 1988 Business Week/Harris Poll asked black and white respondents to estimate the percentage of black people who lived in their neighborhoods (see Table 3). The majority of whites responded that "less than

5 percent" of the people in their neighborhoods were black, while the majority of blacks responded that "over 75 percent" of the people in their neighborhoods were black. From this poll, there is evidence that the concentration of racial groups in United States tends to be homogenous — most blacks say that they live in the same neighborhood where many blacks reside and most whites say that they live in a neighborhood where there are few blacks.

TABLE 3. Percentage of Blacks in Your Neighborhood

January 1988

"If you had to guess, about what percent of the people in your neighborhood would you say are black -- less than 5%, 5-25%, 25-50%, 50-75%, or more than 75% black?"

	Blacks	Whites
Less than 5%	10 %	69 %
5-25%	11	18
25-50%	15	8
50-75%	18	3
Over 75%	45	1
Not sure	1	1

"In the past five years, has the percentage of blacks in your neighborhood gone up, gone down, or stayed the same?

	Blacks	Whites
Gone up	35 %	29 %
Gone down	10	3
Stayed the same	52	61
Not sure	3	7

The Business Week/Harris Poll. (The results of the survey are based on telephone interviews among national cross sections of 1,061 white adults and 531 black adults, 18 and older, contacted during the period January 20-26, 1988.)

About one third of both the black and the white respondents in the January 1988 Business Week/Harris Poll said that there has been an increase in the percentage of blacks in their neighborhoods over the past five years. This perception by the public could reflect the actual increase of the number of blacks in the United States' population (from 1980 to 1990 the number of blacks in the country increased by 3,491,035).

Race issues such as the affirmative action and racial tensions, particularly in the urban America, point to the need to gauge how the public feels about the current state of racial contact, relations and discrimination and the government's handling of race issues in the United States.

In the sections that follow, public opinion polls will be presented on these and other race issues. One caveat when interpreting these polls is that opinions of the minority and white subpopulations are presented in stratified form and are percentages of the corresponding subpopulation. For example, if 74 percent of the black respondents in a particular poll say that they favor affirmative action, one should remember that this number represents a 74 percentage point estimate of the actual black population which comprises 12.1 percent of the total United States' population.

II. RACE RELATIONS AND INTERRACIAL CONTACT

Status of Race Relations in the United States

March 1992

"Generally speaking, do you think race relations in the United States are excellent, good, not-so-good or poor?"

	Whites	Blacks
Excellent	2 %	2 %
Good	32	19
Not-so-good	44	48
Poor	20	30
Don't know	2	1

The Washington Post Poll conducted by ICR Research Services. (The results of the survey are based on telephone interviews with a national sample of 914 whites and 414 blacks, aged 18 and over, contacted during the period February 28-March 3, 1992.)

The Media and Race Relations

March 1992

"Generally speaking, do you think that the news media is helping or hurting race relations in this country?"

	Whites	Blacks
Helping	17 %	22 %
Hurting	60	65
Neither	13	6
Don't know	10	7

"Do you think that the news media focuses too heavily on negative news about blacks, or not?"

	Whites	Blacks
Yes	64 %	80 %
No	25	16
Don't know	11	4

The Washington Post Poll conducted by ICR Research Services. (The results of the survey are based on telephone interviews with a national sample of 914 whites and 414 blacks, aged 18 and over, contacted during the period February 28-March 3, 1992.)

Statements about Race Relations

March 1992

"I am going to read you a few statements and for each I'd like you to tell me whether you tend to agree or disagree with it, or if perhaps you have no opinion about the statement?"

"It is hard for whites and blacks to talk honestly about race relations."

	Whites	Blacks
Agree	47 %	65 %
Disagree	34	31
Don't know	19	4

"It is a bad idea for blacks and whites to marry one another."

	Whites	Blacks
Agree	29 %	16 %
Disagree	46	63
Don't know	25	21

"Blacks too often see racism where it doesn't exist."

	Whites	Blacks
Agree	57 %	34 %
Disagree	19	49
Don't know	24	17

"Most whites have prejudiced views about blacks."

	Whites	Blacks
Agree	48 %	62 %
Disagree	35	27
Don't know	17	11

The Washington Post Poll conducted by ICR Research Services. (The results of the survey are based on telephone interviews with a national sample of 914 whites and 414 blacks, aged 18 and over, contacted during the period February 28-March 3, 1992.)

Contact and Relations Among the Races

May 1991/July 1990

"For each of these three groups [Hispanics, Blacks and Asian-Americans], please tell me how much contact you have with them either where you live, work, or shop--a lot, some, a little, or none at all. (order rotated on every other interview)

Hispanics

	May 1991[1]			July 1990[2]		
	All	Whites	Blacks	All	Whites	Blacks
A lot	25 %	21 %	30 %	26 %	22 %	29 %
Some	23	24	19	23	24	19
A little	30	31	31	29	30	29
None at all	21	23	20	21	23	22
Not sure	1	1	—	1	1	1

Blacks

	May 1991[1]			July 1990[2]		
	All	Whites	Blacks	All	Whites	Blacks
A lot	41 %	37 %	86 %	43 %	38 %	85 %
Some	28	31	9	30	33	8
A little	22	23	4	19	21	6
None at all	8	8	1	7	7	1
Not sure	1	1	—	1	1	—

Asian-Americans

	May 1991[1]			July 1990[2]		
	All	Whites	Blacks	All	Whites	Blacks
A lot	16 %	15 %	18 %	14 %	13 %	18 %
Some	24	25	15	24	25	17
A little	35	34	41	37	37	42
None at all	23	24	26	23	24	20
Not sure	2	2	—	2	2	3

continued on next page

"How would you characterize the relationship between white people and [Hispanics, Blacks and Asian-Americans] -- very good, moderately good, in the middle, not so good, or poor? (order rotated on every other interview.)"

Hispanics

	May 1991[1]			July 1990[2]		
	All	Whites	Blacks	All	Whites	Blacks
Very good	4 %	4 %	2 %	5 %	5 %	5 %
Moderately good	24	25	13	25	27	15
In the middle	32	32	25	35	35	32
Not so good	23	22	33	19	18	27
Poor	9	8	15	7	6	14
Not sure	8	9	12	9	9	7

Blacks

	May 1991[1]			July 1990[2]		
	All	Whites	Blacks	All	Whites	Blacks
Very good	5 %	5 %	—	6 %	7 %	4 %
Moderately good	26	29	11	30	33	16
In the middle	31	31	30	30	30	29
Not so good	23	21	33	21	19	2
Poor	12	10	25	10	7	22
Not sure	3	4	1	3	3	1

Asian-Americans

	May 1991[1]			July 1990[2]		
	All	Whites	Blacks	All	Whites	Blacks
Very good	7 %	7 %	7 %	8 %	8 %	8 %
Moderately good	29	30	24	30	32	23
In the middle	32	32	30	31	31	31
Not so good	15	14	19	14	13	18
Poor	7	7	8	7	6	11
Not sure	10	10	12	10	10	10

---

[1]*The NBC News/Wall Street Journal Poll. (The results of the survey are based on telephone interviews with a national sample of 1,508 adults, 18 and older, contacted during the period May 10-14, 1991.)*

[2]*The NBC News/Wall Street Journal Poll. (The results of the survey are based on telephone interviews with a national sample of 1,555 registered voters, 18 and older, contacted during the period July 6-10, 1990.)*

Comfortable With Interracial Contact?

April 1991

"Which categories apply to you?"*

	Whites	Blacks
Work with many members of another race	51 %	84 %
Uncomfortable working with members of another race	6	17
Worked for a boss of another race	47	92
Uncomfortable working for boss of another race	6	14
Know many members of another race	68	80
Socialize regularly with members of another race	47	63

Newsweek Poll conducted by The Gallup Organization. (The results of the survey are based on telephone interviews with a national sample of 305 blacks and 619 whites contacted during the period April 23-25, 1991. "Don't Know" and other responses not shown.)

**Complete question wording not provided in the press release.*

How Well Are Blacks Treated in Your Community?

June 1990

"In your opinion, how well do you think blacks are treated in your community -- the same as whites are, not very well, or badly?"

	All	Whites	Blacks
The same as whites	63 %	66 %	37 %
Not very well	21	18	43
Badly	3	2	14
No blacks in community	8	8	1
Don't know	5	6	5

The Gallup Poll. (The results of the survey are based on telephone interviews with a national sample of 1,233 adults, aged 18 and over, contacted during the period June 7-10, 1990.)

Interracial Education

June 1990

"Would you, yourself, have any objection to sending your children to a school where a few of the children are black?" (Asked only of whites who have children in school)

Yes	1 %
No	99

"Would you, yourself, have any objection to sending your children to a school where half the children are black?" (Asked only of whites who have children in school)

Yes	10 %
No	87
Don't know	3

"Would you, yourself, have any objection to sending your children to school where more than half of the children are black?" (Asked only of whites who have children in school)

Yes	31 %
No	63
Don't know	6

The Gallup Poll. (The results of the survey are based on telephone interviews with a national sample of 1,233 adults, aged 18 and over, contacted during the period June 7-10, 1990.)

Objections to Sending White Children to School Where Some Children Are Black?

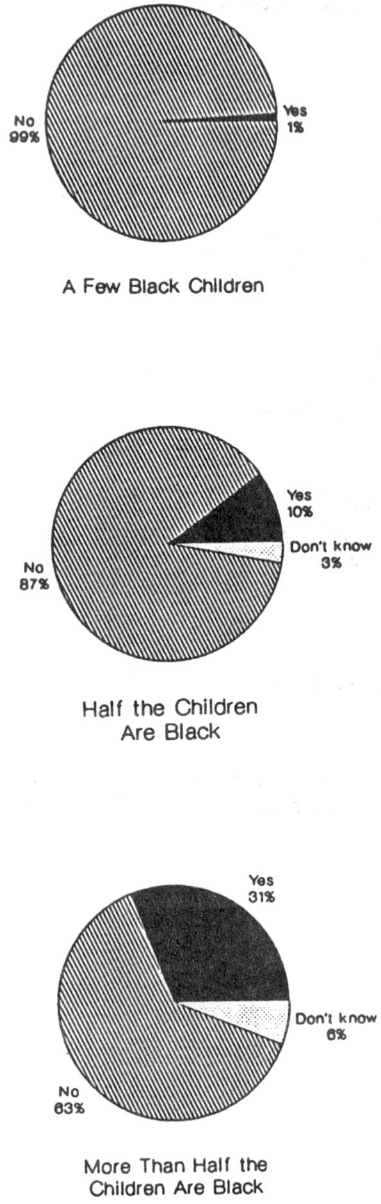

Source: The Gallup Poll, June 1990
Base: Whites who have children in school

Black People as Neighbors

June 1990

"If colored people/black people came to live next door, would you move?" (Asked only of whites--92% of the total sample)

Yes definitely	1 %
Yes, might	4
No, would not move	93
Don't know	2

"Would you move if colored people/black people came to live in great numbers in your neighborhood?" (Asked only of whites--92% of the total sample)

Yes definitely	8 %
Yes, might	18
No, would not move	68
Don't know	6

The Gallup Poll. (The results of the survey are based on telephone interviews with a national sample of 1,233 adults, aged 18 and over, contacted during the period June 7-10, 1990.)

Would Whites Move Out of their Neighborhood if Blacks Moved in?

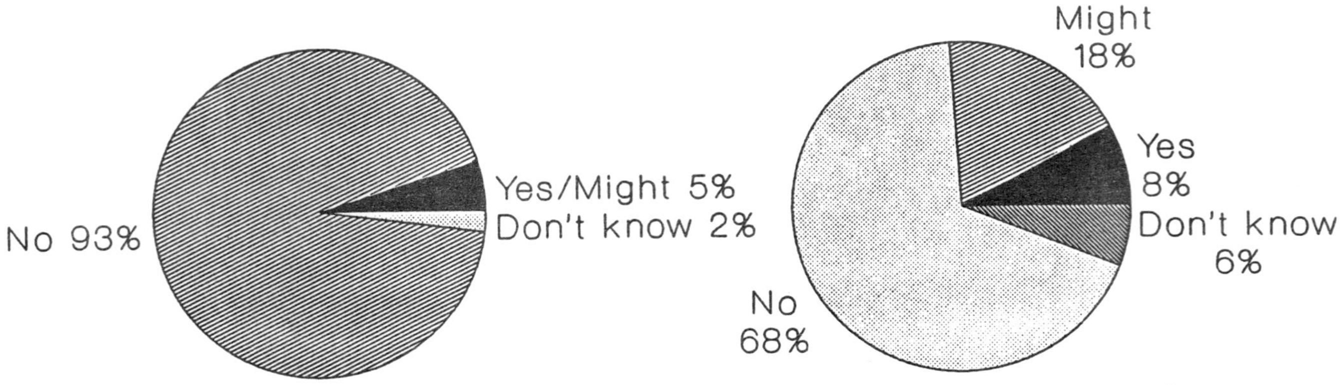

Black People Next Door

Black People in Great Numbers in the Neighborhood

Source: The Gallup Poll, June 1990

Race Relations in the U.S.

May 1990

"Do you think race relations in the United States are generally good or generally bad?"

Generally good	41 %
Generally bad	50
Don't know/No answer	8

The New York Times Poll. (The results of the survey are based on telephone interviews with a national sample of 1,140 adults, aged 18 and older, contacted during the period May 22-24, 1990.)

Desirability as Neighbors

January 1989

"I am going to read you a list of various groups of people. As I read each one, please tell me whether you would or would not like to have them as neighbors."

	Would welcome	Would not	Not sure
Catholics	94 %	3 %	3 %
Protestants	92	5	3
Jews	91	5	4
Blacks	83	12	5
Koreans	79	14	7
Hispanics	78	16	6
Indians, Pakistanis	78	15	7
Vietnamese	75	18	7
Russians	74	19	7
Unmarried couples	71	23	6
Religious fundamentalists	58	30	12
Religious sects, cults	31	62	7

The Gallup Poll. (The results of the survey are based on telephone interviews with a national sample of 1,001 adults, aged 18 and over, contacted during the period January 24-26, 1989—Error=4%.)

Blacks in American Society Treated Fairly?

October 1988

"In general, do you think blacks are treated fairly in American society, or not?"

Yes	47 %
No	45
Not sure	8

The NBC News/Wall Street Journal Poll. (The results of the survey are based on telephone interviews with a national sample of 1,285 voters, 18 and older, contacted during the period October 23-26, 1988.)

Kinds of Racial Contact?

January 1988

"Do you or does anyone in your immediate family work closely with someone who is (black/white), or not?"

	With Whites (asked of black respondents)	With Blacks (asked of white respondents)
Work closely	84 %	59 %
Don't work closely	15	39
Not sure	1	2

"Do you or does that member of your household who works closely with someone who is (black/white) see that person socially frequently, now and then, or almost never?"

	With Whites (asked of black respondents)	With Blacks (asked of white respondents)
Frequently	39 %	27 %
Now and then	23	34
Almost never	35	37
Not sure	3	2

The BusinessWeek/Harris Poll. (The results of the survey are based on telephone interviews among national cross sections of 1,061 white adults and 531 black adults, 18 and older, contacted during the period January 20-26, 1988.)

III. RACIAL PROGRESS

Progress of Race Relations

March 1992

"Do you think race relations here are getting better, getting worse, or staying the same?"

	Whites	Blacks
Better	22 %	15 %
Worse	34	41
About the same	42	42
Don't know	2	2

The Washington Post Poll conducted by ICR Research Services. (The results of the survey are based on telephone interviews with a national sample of 914 whites and 414 blacks, aged 18 and over, contacted during the period February 28-March 3, 1992.)

Statements about the Progress of Blacks

March 1992

"I am going to read you a few statements and for each I'd like you to tell me whether you tend to agree or disagree with it, or if perhaps you have no opinion about the statement?"

"Black people are not achieving equally as fast as they could because many whites don't want them to get ahead."

	Whites	Blacks
Agree	35 %	71 %
Disagree	45	19
Don't know	20	10

"Almost all the gains made by blacks in recent years have come at the expense of whites."

	Whites	Blacks
Agree	11 %	20 %
Disagree	66	58
Don't know	23	22

continued on next page

"If blacks would try harder, they could be just as well off as whites."

	Whites	Blacks
Agree	38 %	52 %
Disagree	35	39
Don't know	27	9

"Over the past few years, blacks have gotten more economically than they deserve."

	Whites	Blacks
Agree	15 %	8 %
Disagree	65	85
Don't know	20	7

The Washington Post Poll conducted by ICR Research Services. (The results of the survey are based on telephone interviews with a national sample of 914 whites and 414 blacks, aged 18 and over, contacted during the period February 28-March 3, 1992.)

Quality of Life for Blacks in Last 10 Years

June 1991/June 1990

"Looking back over the last 10 years, do you think the quality of life of blacks has gotten better, stayed about the same, or gotten worse?"

	June 1991[1]			June 1990[2]		
	All	Whites	Blacks	All	Whites	Blacks
Gotten better	53 %	55 %	35 %	61 %	62 %	46 %
Stayed same	27	27	26	24	25	25
Gotten worse	15	13	36	8	6	23
Don't know	5	5	3	7	7	6

[1]*The Gallup Poll. (The results of the survey are based on telephone interviews with a national sample of 990 adults, aged 18 and over, contacted during the period June 13-16, 1991—Error=4%)*

[2]*The Gallup Poll. (The results of the survey are based on telephone interviews with a national sample of 1,233 adults, aged 18 and over, contacted during the period June 7-10, 1990.)*

Quality of Life for Blacks In the Last 10 Years

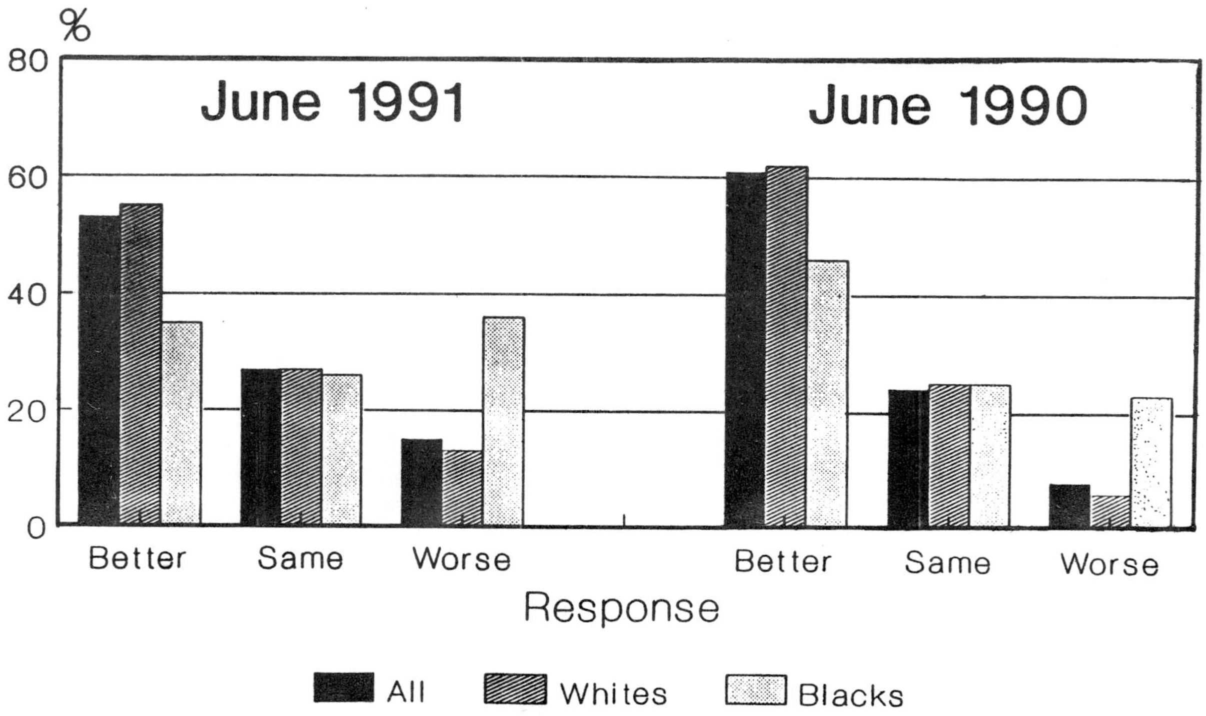

Source: The Gallup Poll

Chances for Blacks in Your Community

June 1991/June 1990/December 1989

"For the next few questions, I'd like you to think about your own community. In general, do you think blacks have as good a chance as white people in your community to get any kind of job for which they are qualified, or don't you think they have as good a chance?"

	June 1991[1]			June 1990[2]		
	All	Whites	Blacks	All	Whites	Blacks
Blacks have as good a chance	68 %	70 %	40 %	70 %	73 %	43 %
Blacks do not have as good a chance as whites	26	23	58	23	20	54
No blacks/whites in community (volunteered)	4	4	-	3	4	-
Don't know	2	3	2	4	-	-

	Dec 1989[3]
Blacks have as good a chance	65 %
Blacks do not have as good a chance as whites	28
No blacks/whites in community (volunteered)	5
Don't know	2

"Do you think blacks have as good a chance as white people in your community to get any kind of housing they can afford, or don't they have as good a chance?"

	June 1991[1]			June 1990[2]		
	All	Whites	Blacks	All	Whites	Blacks
Blacks have as good a chance	72 %	74 %	55 %	72 %	75 %	47 %
Blacks do not have as good a chance as whites	23	21	42	19	16	46
No blacks/whites in community (volunteered)	3	3	1	3	4	-
Don't know	2	2	2	6	5	7

continued on next page

	Dec 1989[3]
Blacks have as good a chance	68 %
Blacks do not have as good a chance as whites	27
No blacks/whites in community (volunteered)	3
Don't know	2

"Do you think black children have as good a chance as white children in your community to get a good education, or don't they have as good a chance?"

	June 1991[1]			June 1990[2]		
	All	Whites	Blacks	All	Whites	Blacks
Black children have as good a chance	81 %	83 %	56 %	83 %	85 %	68 %
Black children do not have as good a chance as whites	15	13	38	11	9	29
No blacks/whites in community (volunteered)	2	2		3	4	1
Don't know	2	2	6	3	2	2

	Dec 1989[3]
Blacks children have as good a chance	80 %*
Blacks children do not have as good a chance as whites	15
No blacks/whites in community (volunteered)	4
Don't know	1

---

[1]*The Gallup Poll. (The results of the survey are based on telephone interviews with a national sample of 990 adults, aged 18 and over, contacted during the period June 13-16, 1991—Error=4%.)*

[2]*The Gallup Poll. (The results of the survey are based on telephone interviews with a national sample of 1,233 adults, aged 18 and over, contacted during the period June 7-10, 1990.)*

[3]*The Gallup Poll. (The results of the survey are based on personal interviews with a national sample of 1,235 adults, aged 18 and over, contacted during the period December 7-10, 1989.)*

**Varied question wording: "Do you think black children have as good a chance as white children in your community to get a good education, or don't you think they have as good a chance?"*

Chances for Blacks in Your Community -- Comparison with Whites

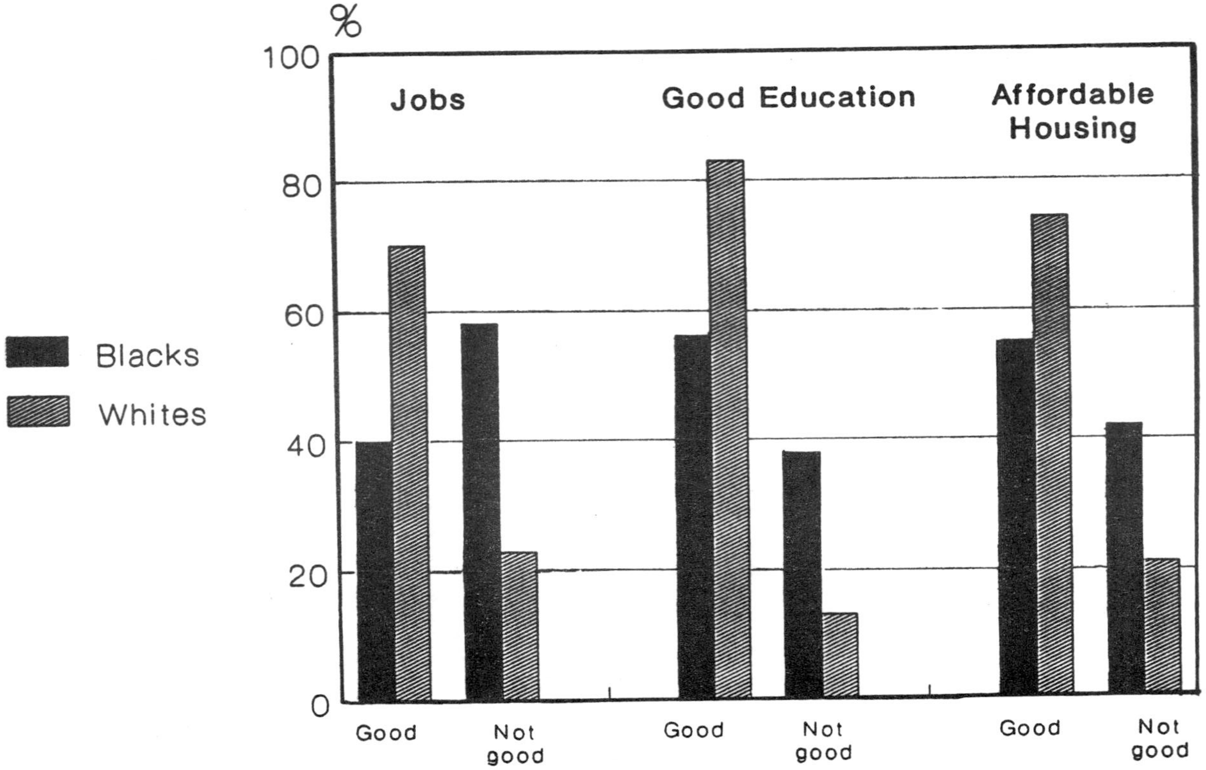

Source: The Gallup Poll, June 1991

Progress in Area of Civil Rights Over Past Year?

June 1991/June 1990/December 1989

"Over the past year or so, how much progress do you think has been made in the area of civil rights in this country--a lot of progress, some progress, not very much progress, or no progress at all?"

	June 1991[1]		
	All	Whites	Blacks
A lot of progress	11 %	11 %	7 %
Some progress	47	49	31
Not very much progress	27	26	35
No progress at all	11	10	25
Don't know	4	4	2

	June 1990[2]	December 1989[3]
	All	All
A lot of progress	16 %	11 %
Some progress	48	44
Not very much progress	23	30
No progress at all	9	12
Don't know	4	3

[1]*The Gallup Poll. (The results of the survey are based on telephone interviews with a national sample of 990 adults, aged 18 and over, contacted during the period June 13-16, 1991—Error=4%.)*

[2]*The Gallup Poll. (The results of the survey are based on telephone interviews with a national sample of 1,233 adults, aged 18 and over, contacted during the period June 7-10, 1990.)*

[3]*The Gallup Poll. (The results of the survey are based on personal interviews with a national sample of 1,235 adults, aged 18 and over, contacted during the period December 7-10, 1989.)*

Have Job Opportunities Become Better for Blacks?

May 1991

"Have job opportunities for blacks become better in the past five years?"

	Whites	Blacks
Better	64 %	39 %
Worse	5	22
Haven't changed	26	37

Time/CNN Poll conducted by Yankelovich, Clancy & Shulman. (The results of the survey are based on telephone interviews with a national sample of 504 white and 504 black adults, 18 and older, contacted during the period May 24-29, 1991.)

Could Racial Disturbances of 1960s Happen Again?

May 1991

"Do you think the widespread racial disturbances that occurred in this country during the 1960s could happen again now, or have conditions changed enough so that such disturbances are now unlikely?"

	All	Whites	Blacks
Disturbances could occur now	57 %	56 %	66 %
Disturbances unlikely now	39	40	29
Not sure	4	4	5

The NBC News/Wall Street Journal Poll. (The results of the survey are based on telephone interviews with a national sample of 1,508 adults, 18 and older, contacted during the period May 10-14, 1991.)

America's Ability to Ensure Rights to Minorities

May 1991

"Now here are some questions about whether you are satisfied or dissatisfied with various things about America today. Are you satisfied or dissatisfied with each of the following: -- The nation's ability to ensure the rights of its racial and ethnic minorities?"

Satisfied	46 %
Dissatisfied	50
Don't know	4

"In your opinion, which nation do you consider the world leader in the following areas: -- Ability to ensure the rights of its racial and ethnic minorities?"

U.S. is world leader	69 %
Any mention of any other country as leader	12
Don't know	20

The Gallup Poll. (The results of the survey are based on telephone interviews with a national sample of 1,003 adults, 18 and older, contacted during the period May 23-26, 1991—Error=4%.)

Have Race Relations Gotten Better in the Past Five Years?

May 1991/July 1990

"Over the course of the past five years, do you feel that race relations between blacks and whites have gotten better, worse, or stayed about the same?"

	May 1991[1]			July 1990[2]		
	All	Whites	Blacks	All	Whites	Blacks
Better	38 %	40 %	20 %	37 %	38 %	26 %
Worse	22	20	39	22	20	35
Stayed about the same	38	38	40	39	40	35
Not sure	2	2	1	2	2	4

[1]*The NBC News/Wall Street Journal Poll. (The results of the survey are based on telephone interviews with a national sample of 1,508 adults, 18 and older, contacted during the period May 10-14, 1991.)*

[2]*The NBC News/Wall Street Journal Poll. (The results of the survey are based on telephone interviews with a national sample of 1,555 registered voters, 18 and older, contacted during the period July 6-10, 1990.)*

Are Blacks Better Off Now than Ten Years Ago?

May 1991/July 1990

"Compared to 10 years ago, do you think blacks in America are a lot better off, a little better off, about the same, a little worse off, or a lot worse off?"

May 1991[1]

	All	Whites	Blacks
A lot better off	24 %	26 %	7 %
A little better off	43	43	41
About the same	17	18	15
A little worse off	9	8	19
A lot worse off	4	2	15
Not sure	3	3	3

July 1990[2]

	All	Whites	Blacks
A lot better off	23 %	24 %	16 %
A little better off	45	45	44
About the same	19	19	11
A little worse off	8	7	18
A lot worse off	2	1	11
Not sure	3	3	0

---

[1] *The NBC News/Wall Street Journal Poll. (The results of the survey are based on telephone interviews with a national sample of 1,508 adults, 18 and older, contacted during the period May 10-14, 1991.)*

[2] *The NBC News/Wall Street Journal Poll. (The results of the survey are based on telephone interviews with a national sample of 1,555 registered voters, 18 and older, contacted during the period July 6-10, 1990.)*

Progress of the Nation -- Race Relations

March 1991

"Now I want to ask you about a few issues facing the country. Please tell me whether you think the country is making enough progress or is not making enough progress on each one. -- Race relations"

Enough	47 %
Not enough	46
No problem	3
Don't know/No answer	4

The ABC/News Washington Post Poll. (The results of the survey are based on telephone interviews with a sample of 1,215 adults, 18 and older, contacted within the continental United States during the period March 1-4, 1991.)

Getting Out of Poverty for a Black Person Today and Ten Years Ago

December 1990

"What if a person is black? Compared to ten years ago, do you think it is easier today or harder today for a black person to start out poor, work hard, and to get out of poverty?"

Easier	55 %
Harder	31
Same	8
Don't know/No answer	7

The New York Times Poll. (The results of the survey are based on telephone interviews with a national sample of 1,028 adults, aged 18 and older, contacted during the period December 12-14, 1990.)

Racial Attitudes In American Society

June 1990

"Now, thinking about American society as a whole, do you think society has become more tolerant of people of different colors and races lately, less tolerant, or has it not changed?"

	All	Whites	Blacks
More tolerant	51 %	54 %	29 %
Less tolerant	17	16	29
Has not changed	26	24	35
Don't know	6	6	6

The Gallup Poll. (The results of the survey are based on telephone interviews with a national sample of 1,233 adults, aged 18 and over, contacted during the period June 7-10, 1990.)

Position of Blacks Changed a Lot in Past Few Years?

May 1990

"In the past few years we have heard a lot about improving the position of black people in this country. How much real change do you think there has been in the position of black people in the past few years, a lot, some, or not much at all?"

A lot	40 %
Some	43
Not much at all	15
Don't know/No answer	2

The New York Times/CBS News Poll. (The results of the survey are based on telephone interviews with a national sample of 1,140 adults, aged 18 and older, contacted during the period May 22-24, 1990.)

Major Domestic Issues in Next Ten Years -- Race Problems

January 1990

"Now I'm going to read to you a list of problems. For each, please tell me whether this problem will get better, get worse or stay about the same in the next 10 years. Here's the first: Racism, racial prejudice" (Asked only of 1/2 the total sample)

Get better	45 %
Get worse	22
Stay about the same	33
Don't know/No opinion	-

The ABC News/Washington Post Poll. (The results of the survey are based on telephone interviews with a sample of 1,518 adults, 18 and older, contacted within the continental United States during the period January 11-15, 1990.)

Do You Think Predjudice Will Decline?

December 1989

"Let me ask you if you think each of these things will happen in your lifetime. Do you think a decline in prejudice will happen in your lifetime, or not?"

Will happen	49 %
Will not happen	47
Not sure	4

The Harris Survey. (The results of the survey are based on telephone interviews with a national sample of 1,251 adults, aged 18 and over, contacted during the period December 6-10, 1989.)

Will Better Living Standards of Blacks Hurt Living Standards of Whites?

December 1989

"Do you think further improvements in the standard of living of blacks in general will reduce the standard of living of whites, or do you think that the situation of blacks can improve without hurting the situation of whites?"

Improvement in black standard of living will hurt whites	12 %
Black standard of living can improve and not hurt whites	82
Don't know	6

The Gallup Poll. (The results of the survey are based on personal interviews with a national sample of 1,235 adults, aged 18 and over, contacted during the period December 7-10, 1989.)

Will an Improvement in Black Living Standards Hurt White Living Standards?

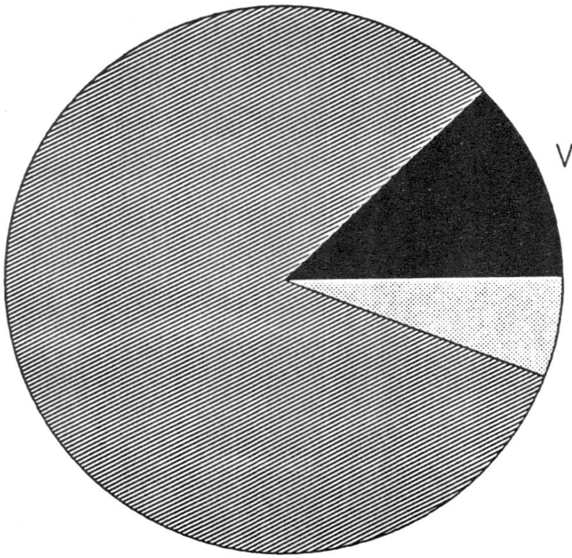

Source: The Gallup Poll, December 1989

Do You Expect Equality for Blacks in Your Lifetime?

December 1989

"Let me ask you if you think each of these things will happen in your lifetime. Do you think equality for blacks will happen in your lifetime, or not?

Will happen	55 %
Will not happen	40
Not sure	5

The Harris Survey. (The results of the survey are based on telephone interviews with a national sample of 1,251 adults, aged 18 and over, contacted during the period December 6-10, 1989.)

Attention to Civil Rights By Groups

December 1989

"For each of the following groups I read, please tell me whether you think there has been too much attention or not enough attention to the civil rights of this group."

	Too much attention	Not enough attention	Right amount of attention	Don't know/No answer
Black people	39 %	40 %	17 %	4 %
Asian-Americans	25	45	17	13
Women	29	49	18	4
The Elderly	4	84	10	2
Disabled and handicapped people	6	81	11	2
Hispanics	28	46	15	11
People who have the disease AIDS	31	51	13	5
Jewish people	20	43	22	15

The Gallup Poll. (The results of the survey are based on personal interviews with a national sample of 1,235 adults, aged 18 and over, contacted during the period December 7-10, 1989.)

Social Indicators by the Year 2000 -- Racial Tensions

November 1989

"For each of the following social conditions, please tell me whether you think it will increase or decrease by the year 2000. -- Tensions between racial and ethnic groups"

Increase	39 %
Decrease	52
Same	6
Don't know	3

The Gallup Poll. (The results of the survey are based on telephone interviews with a national sample of 1,234 adults, aged 18 and over, contacted during the period November 16-19, 1989.)

Will Race Relations in the U.S. Improve?

July 1989

"Do you think that race relations in the United States will improve, decline, or stay about the same during the 1990s?"

	Total	Whites	Blacks	Other
Improve	44 %	44 %	40 %	41 %
Stay about the same	44	44	45	43
Decline	13	12	15	14
Don't Know/No answer	-	-	-	2

The Hearst Corporation Survey presented at the National Convention of the Society of Professional Journalists. (The results of the survey are based on telephone interviews with a random sample of 1,001 residents of the U.S. contacted during the period June 19 - July 9, 1989.)

Black Progress in the Past 30 Years

January 1988

"It's been said that blacks in America have made considerable economic and social progress over the past 30 years. Do you feel that blacks have the same opportunities to live a middle class life as whites, or don't you feel that has happened?

	Blacks	Whites
Yes, blacks have same opportunities	50 %	70 %
No, do not have same opportunities	46	27
Not sure	4	3

"If you had to say, which of these do you feel has been most responsible for what progress blacks have made over the past 30 years -- individual initiative by blacks, a decline in white discrimination against blacks, government laws against discrimination, companies really trying to hire blacks, or pressure from civil rights organizations?"

	Blacks	Whites
Individual initiative by blacks	21 %	25 %
A decline in white discrimination	7	12
Government laws against discrimination	18	25
Companies trying to hire blacks	11	8
Pressure from civil rights groups	35	18
No progress made by blacks (volunteered)	-	-
Not sure	8	12

The BusinessWeek/Harris Poll. (The results of the survey are based on telephone interviews among national cross sections of 1,061 white adults and 531 black adults, 18 and older, contacted during the period January 20-26, 1988.)

Are Blacks More Vulnerable to Economic Changes than Whites?

January 1988

"Do you feel that blacks are more vulnerable than whites to changes in individual companies, industries, or the economy, less vulnerable, or not much different from whites?"

	Blacks	Whites
More vulnerable	33 %	24 %
Less vulnerable	10	8
Not much different	52	60
Not sure	5	8

The BusinessWeek/Harris Poll. (The results of the survey are based on telephone interviews among national cross sections of 1,061 white adults and 531 black adults, 18 and older, contacted during the period January 20-26, 1988.)

Has American Society Become More or Less Racist?

January 1988

"Finally, do you think that during the 1980s, American society has become more or less racist?"

	Blacks	Whites
More racist	37 %	20 %
Less racist	54	70
No change (volunteered)	6	6
Not sure	3	4

The BusinessWeek/Harris Poll. (The results of the survey are based on telephone interviews among national cross sections of 1,061 white adults and 531 black adults, 18 and older, contacted during the period January 20-26, 1988.)

IV. DISCRIMINATION

A. DISCRIMINATION IN THE WORKPLACE

Agree or Disagree That Discrimination Is Not a Problem?

March 1992

"I am going to read you a few statements and for each I'd like you to tell me whether you tend to agree or disagree with it, or if perhaps you have no opinion about the statement. ...Discrimination against blacks is no longer a problem in the United States?"

	Whites	Blacks
Agree	10 %	9 %
Disagree	79	85
Don't know	11	6

The Washington Post Poll conducted by ICR Research Services. (The results of the survey are based on telephone interviews with a national sample of 914 whites and 414 blacks, aged 18 and over, contacted during the period February 28-March 3, 1992.)

Have You Ever Been Discriminated Against?*

September 1991

"Have you:"

	Whites	Blacks	Latinos
Personally been discriminated against in job/education?	21 %	51 %	43 %
Experienced "reverse discrimination"?	14	16	13

The Los Angeles Times Poll. (The results of the survey are based on telephone interviews with a national sample of 1,623 adults, aged 18 and over, contacted during the period September 21-25, 1991.)

*The exact question wording is not provided by the print source.

Discrimination in Employment and Promotions

September 1991

"Do you think there is a lot of discrimination against blacks in employment today, some discrimination, or not very much discrimination?"

	All	Whites	Blacks
A lot	19 %	13 %	53 %
Some	45	47	35
Not very much	31	34	8
Don't know/No answer	5	6	4

"Have you ever been discriminated against in getting a job or promotion because of your race?"

Yes	11 %
No	88
Don't know/No answer	2

The CBS News/New York Times Poll. (The results of the survey are based on telephone interviews with a national sample of 1,519 adults, aged 18 and older, contacted during the period September 3-5, 1991.)

Ever Been Discriminated Against for Your Race?

June 1991

"Have you ever been discriminated against in getting a job or promotion because of your race?"

Yes	11 %
No	89
Don't Know/No Answer	1

The CBS News/New York Times Poll. (The results of the survey are based on telephone interviews with a national sample of 1,424 adults, 18 and older, contacted during the period June 3-6, 1991.)

Are Minorities Discriminated Against in Hiring?

June 1991

"Do you think blacks and other minorities are discriminated against in hiring, or not?"

Yes	49 %
No	48
Don't know/No opinion	2

The ABC News/Washington Post Poll. (The results of the survey are based on telephone interviews with a sample of 1,511 adults, 18 and older, contacted within the continental United States during the period May 30-June 2, 1991.)

Black or White More Likely To Be Hired?

June 1991

"Suppose a black and a white were competing for the same job and both were equally qualified. Generally, do you think the black applicant will be more or less likely to be hired?"

More likely	32 %
Less likely	50
No difference (volunteered)	9
Don't know/No opinion	9

"Is that a good thing or a bad thing?"

Black more likely hired	
Good thing	9 %
Bad thing	17
Neither good nor bad (volunteered)	5
Don't know/No opinion	1
Black less likely hired	
Good thing	2 %
Bad thing	44
Neither good nor bad (volunteered)	2
Don't know/No opinion	1
No difference	
Good thing	7 %
Bad thing	-
Neither good nor bad (volunteered)	1
Don't know/No opinion	-
Don't know/No opinion	9

The ABC News/Washington Post Poll. (The results of the survey are based on telephone interviews with a sample of 1,511 adults, 18 and older, contacted within the continental United States during the period May 30-June 2, 1991.)

Discrimination's Role in Job Advancement

June 1991

"When it comes to advancing to management or supervisory positions do you think blacks have a better chance than whites, a worse chance, or what?"

Better chance	13 %
Same (volunteered)	23
Worse chance	58
Don't know/No opinion	6

"Is that because of racial discrimination or some other reason?" (Asked only of those who think blacks have a better chance of advancing to management than whites--13% of the total sample)

Racial discrimination	65 %
Some other reason	32
Don't know/No opinion	3

"Is that because of racial discrimination or some other reason?" (Asked only of those who think blacks have a worse change of advancing to management than whites--58% of the total sample)

Racial discrimination	73 %
Some other reason	23
Don't know/No opinion	3

The ABC News/Washington Post Poll. (The results of the survey are based on telephone interviews with a sample of 1,511 adults, 18 and older, contacted within the continental United States during the period May 30–June 2, 1991.)

Do Blacks Have a Better or Worse Chance at Job Advancement than Whites?

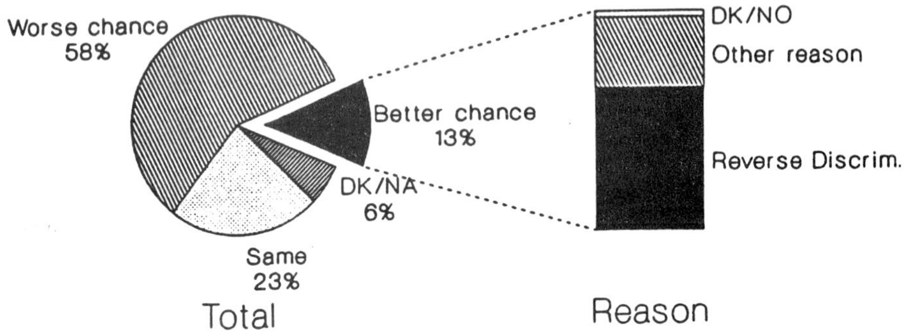

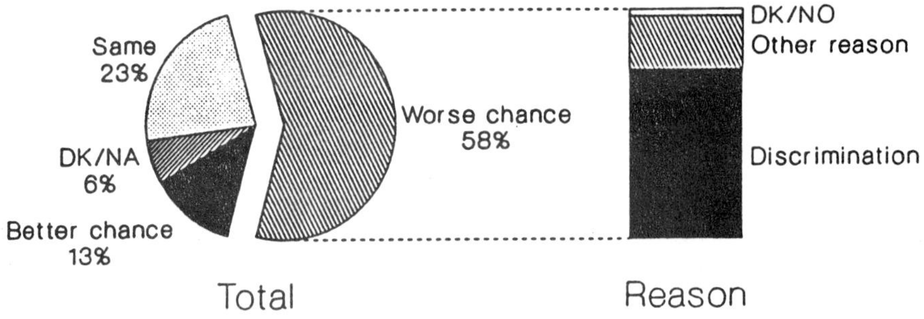

Source: The ABC News/Washington Post Poll
June 1991

Do Employers Practice Discrimination?

June 1990

"Do you believe that, in general, employers practice some form of discrimination in their hiring or promotion practices, regardless of their official policies?"

All or most	51 %
Some	27
No or small	19
Don't know	4

The National Law Journal/Lexis Poll. (The results of the survey are based on telephone interviews with a national sample of 803 adults, 18 and older, contacted in June 1990—error not shown by source.)

Will Black or White Be Hired if Both are Equally Qualified?

January 1988

"Suppose a black and a white were competing for the same job and both were equally qualified. Generally, do you think the black will be more or less likely to be hired?"

	Blacks	Whites
More likely	10 %	32 %
Less likely	80	37
No difference (volunteered)	5	14
Not sure	5	17

The BusinessWeek/Harris Poll. (The results of the survey are based on telephone interviews among national cross sections of 1,061 white adults and 531 black adults, 18 and older, contacted during the period January 20-26, 1988.)

Chances of Job Advancement for Blacks as Good as for Whites?

January 1988

"Do you feel that the chances for blacks to advance to managerial or supervisory positions generally are as good as those for whites, or not?"

	Blacks	Whites
As good a chance	34 %	53 %
Not as good a chance	62	41
A better chance (volunteered)	1	1
Not sure	3	5

The BusinessWeek/Harris Poll. (The results of the survey are based on telephone interviews among national cross sections of 1,061 white adults and 531 black adults, 18 and older, contacted during the period January 20-26, 1988.)

Are Blacks Treated Better in the Workplace than in Society?

January 1988

"If you had to say, do you feel that blacks are treated more fairly in the workplace than they are in society as a whole, or don't you feel that is so?

	Blacks	Whites
Yes, treated more fairly	39 %	54 %
No, not so	50	27
Treated the same in both	5	11
Not sure	6	8

The BusinessWeek/Harris Poll. (The results of the survey are based on telephone interviews among national cross sections of 1,061 white adults and 531 black adults, 18 and older, contacted during the period January 20-26, 1988.)

Are Blacks Paid as Much as Whites for Doing the Same Job?

January 1988

"Do you feel that most blacks are paid the same as whites who are doing the same job, or do you feel they are paid less?

	Blacks	Whites
Paid the same	40 %	70 %
Paid less	53	18
Paid more (volunteered)	1	1
Not sure	6	11

The BusinessWeek/Harris Poll. (The results of the survey are based on telephone interviews among national cross sections of 1,061 white adults and 531 black adults, 18 and older, contacted during the period January 20-26, 1988.)

B. POLICIES DESIGNED TO REDUCE DISCRIMINATION

1. Racial Policies in Society

Affirmative Action Proposals

November 1991

"I'm going to read you some proposals that are being discussed around the country today. As I read each proposal, please tell me whether you would favor or oppose it. First..."

	All Respondents		
	Favor	Oppose	Don't Know
Busing children to achieve better racial balance in the public schools	38 %	58 %	4 %
Giving blacks preference over equally qualified whites in such matters as getting into college or getting jobs because of past discrimination against blacks	20	76	4

The Gallup Poll. (The results of the survey are based on telephone interviews with a national sample of 1,011 adults, aged 18 and over, contacted during the period November 7-10, 1991.)

Affirmative Action*

September 1991

"Do you...

	Whites	Blacks	Latinos
—favor affirmative action for minorities?"	50 %	74 %	72 %
—oppose affirmative action?"	22	6	10
—think affirmative action goes too far?"	28	4	10
—think it doesn't go far enough?"	21	60	44
—think it is often unfair to others?"	33	22	20
—think it is seldom unfair?"	57	72	69
"Have you...			
—received job/educational chance because of affirmative action?"	4	20	22
—got an affirmative action program at work/school?"	35	36	31

The Los Angeles Times Poll. (The results of the survey are based on telephone interviews with a national sample of 1,623 adults, aged 18 and over, contacted during the period September 21-25, 1991.)

*The exact question wording is not provided by the print source.

Educational Requirements for Workers

September 1991

"The Bush administration says that employers should be allowed to impose educational requirements greater than the job really requires -- like a high school diploma for a janitor -- in order to encourage young people to finish high school. Critics say this would result in discrimination against older workers who didn't finish high school. Do you think employers should, or should not be allowed to impose educational requirements that do not relate to the duties of the job?"

	Total	Whites	Blacks
Should	31 %	29 %	36 %
Should not	64	66	56
Don't know/No answer	5	5	8

The CBS News/New York Times Poll. (The results of the survey are based on telephone interviews with a national sample of 1,519 adults, aged 18 and older, contacted during the period September 3-5, 1991.)

Job Preference To Make Up For Past Discrimination

September 1991

"Do you believe that where there has been job discrimination against blacks in the past, preference in hiring should be given to blacks today?"

Yes, preference	20 %
No	60
Depends	15
Don't know/No answer	5

The CBS News/New York Times Poll. (The results of the survey are based on telephone interviews with a national sample of 1,519 adults, aged 18 and older, contacted during the period September 3-5, 1991.)

Meaning of "Affirmative Action"

September 1991

"Do you think "affirmative action" for blacks and women always means quotas, or do you think it is possible to have affirmative action without quotas?"

	All	Whites	Blacks
Means quotas	21 %	22 %	16 %
Possible without	59	59	60
Don't know/No answer	20	19	24

The CBS News/New York Times Poll. (The results of the survey are based on telephone interviews with a national sample of 1,519 adults, aged 18 and older, contacted during the period September 3-5, 1991.)

Reactions to the Terms "Racial Job Preference" and "Affirmative Action"

June 1991

"When you hear the phrase "racial job preference," what comes to mind? What else?"

Positive	
Equal opportunities for minorities to get jobs	6 %
Equal job opportunities for those qualified	5
Affirmative action	2
Negative	
Reverse discrimination	22
Racism	14
Job preference by race	11
Hiring minorities even if they have lower qualifications	10
Hiring minorities to meet quotas	9
Not sure	17
All other responses	4

"When you hear the phrase "affirmative action," what comes to mind? What else?"

Positive	
Positive action/doing something good	13 %
Equality between the races/ equal rights	8
Equal job opportunities for minorities regardless of color or creed	6
Equal job opportunities for women	2
Negative	
Race quotas	6
Reverse discrimination	6
Not sure	30
All other responses	29

The Harris Survey. (The results of the survey are based on interview with a national sample of 1,253 adults, aged 18 and over, contacted during the period June 20-24, 1991.)

How People View the Words "Racial Preference" and "Affirmative Action"

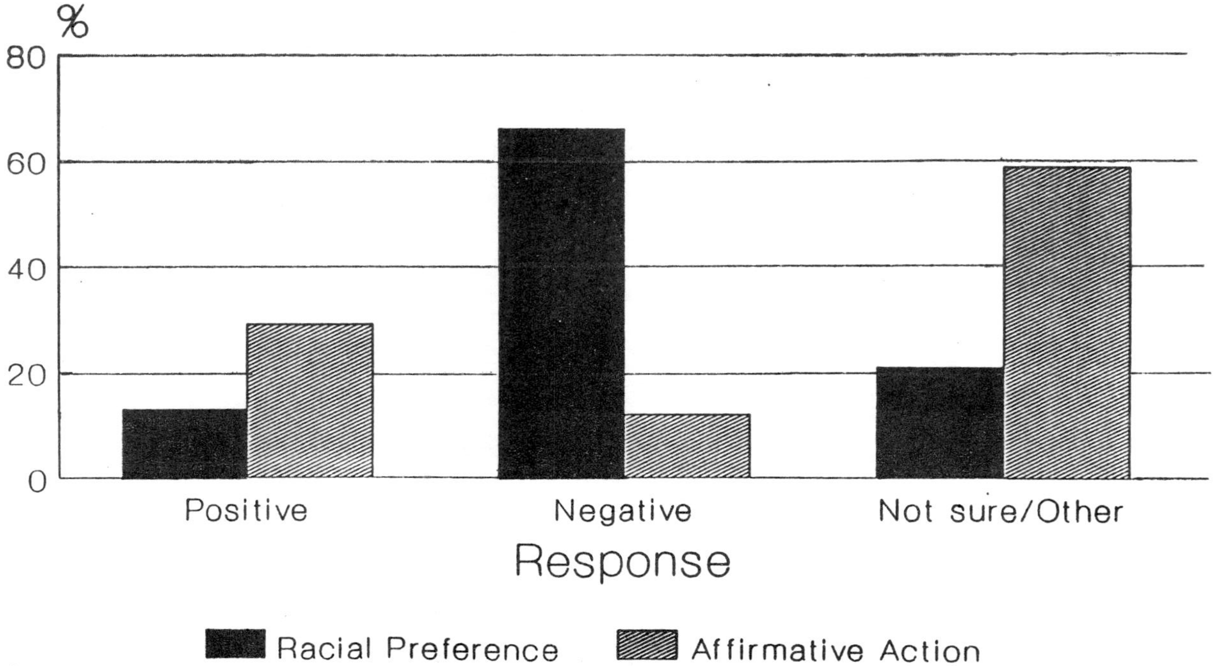

Source: The Harris Survey, June 1991

Familiar with Term "Racial Quotas"?

June 1991

"Are you familiar with the term "racial quotas"?

Familiar	73 %
Unfamiliar	26
Not sure	1

The NBC News/Wall Street Journal Poll. (The results are based on telephone interviews with a national sample of 1,006 registered voters contacted during the period June 22-25, 1991—Error=4%)

Require Companies to Have Quotas?

June 1991

"Generally speaking, do you think that companies should be required to hire about the same proportion of blacks and other minorities as live in the surrounding community, or not?"

	All	Whites	Blacks
Yes, should be required	45 %	41 %	78 %
Should not be required	50	54	17
Don't know	5	5	6

The Gallup Poll. (The results of the survey are based on telephone interviews with a national sample of 990 adults, aged 18 and over, contacted during the period June 13-16, 1991—Error=4%.)

Require Companies to Hire Proportionally to the Population?

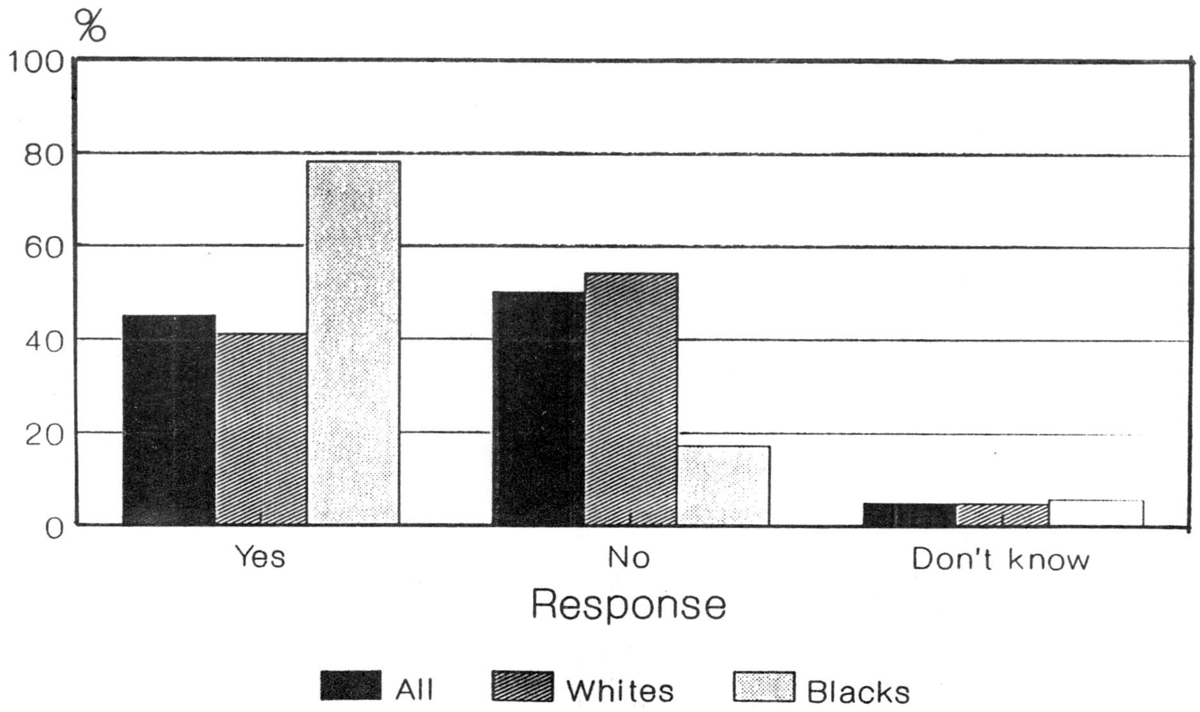

Source: The Gallup Poll, June 1991

Preferential Treatment for Blacks and Minorities

June 1991

"Do you think blacks and other minorities should receive preference in hiring to make up for past inequalities, or not?"

Yes	17 %
No	80
Don't Know	3

"How about if there are no rigid quotas for hiring by race -- then do you think blacks and other minorities should receive preference in hiring to make up for past inequalities, or not?" (Asked only of those who do not think blacks and other minorities should receive preferential treatment or those who don't know--83% of the total sample)

Yes	10 %
No	86
Don't know/No opinion	4

The ABC News/Washington Post Poll. (The results of the survey are based on telephone interviews with a sample of 1,511 adults, 18 and older, contacted within the continental United States during the period May 30-June 2, 1991.)

Hiring Preference for Blacks and Minorities

June 1991

"Do you think blacks and other minorities should or should not receive hiring preference to make up for past discrimination against them?"

	All	Whites	Blacks
Should	18 %	12 %	51 %
Should not	78	84	42
Not sure	4	4	7

The NBC News/Wall Street Journal Poll. (The results are based on telephone interviews with a national sample of 1,006 registered voters contacted during the period June 22-25, 1991—Error=4%.)

Does Preference in Hiring for Blacks Hurt Whites?

June 1991

"When preference in hiring is given to blacks, do you think in the long run this helps whites, hurts whites, or doesn't affect whites much one way or the other?"

Helps	4 %
Hurts	40
Doesn't affect	47
Don't know/No answer	10

The New York Times Poll. (The results of the survey are based on telephone interviews with a national sample of 1,424 adults, aged 18 and older, contacted during the period June 3-6, 1991.)

Favor or Oppose Affirmative Action?

June 1991/May 1991/July 1990

"All in all, do you favor or oppose affirmative action programs in business for blacks and other minority groups?"

	June 1991[1]		
	All	Whites	Blacks
Favor	59 %	55 %	82 %
Oppose	29	32	12
Not sure	11	12	6

	May 1991[2]		
	All	Whites	Blacks
Favor	57 %	52 %	86 %
Oppose	33	37	10
Not sure	10	11	4

	July 1990[3]		
	All	Whites	Blacks
Favor	68 %	66 %	84 %
Oppose	18	19	9
Not sure	14	15	7

[1]*The NBC News/Wall Street Journal Poll. (The results of the survey are based on telephone interviews with a national sample of 1,006 registered voters, contacted during the period June 22-25, 1991—Error=4%.)*

[2]*The NBC News/Wall Street Journal Poll. (The results of the survey are based on telephone interviews with a national sample of 1,508 adults, 18 and older, contacted during the period May 10-14, 1991.)*

[3]*The NBC News/Wall Street Journal Poll. (The results of the survey are based on telephone interviews with a national sample of 1,555 registered voters, 18 and older, contacted during the period July 6-10, 1990.)*

Those Who Favor Affirmative Action

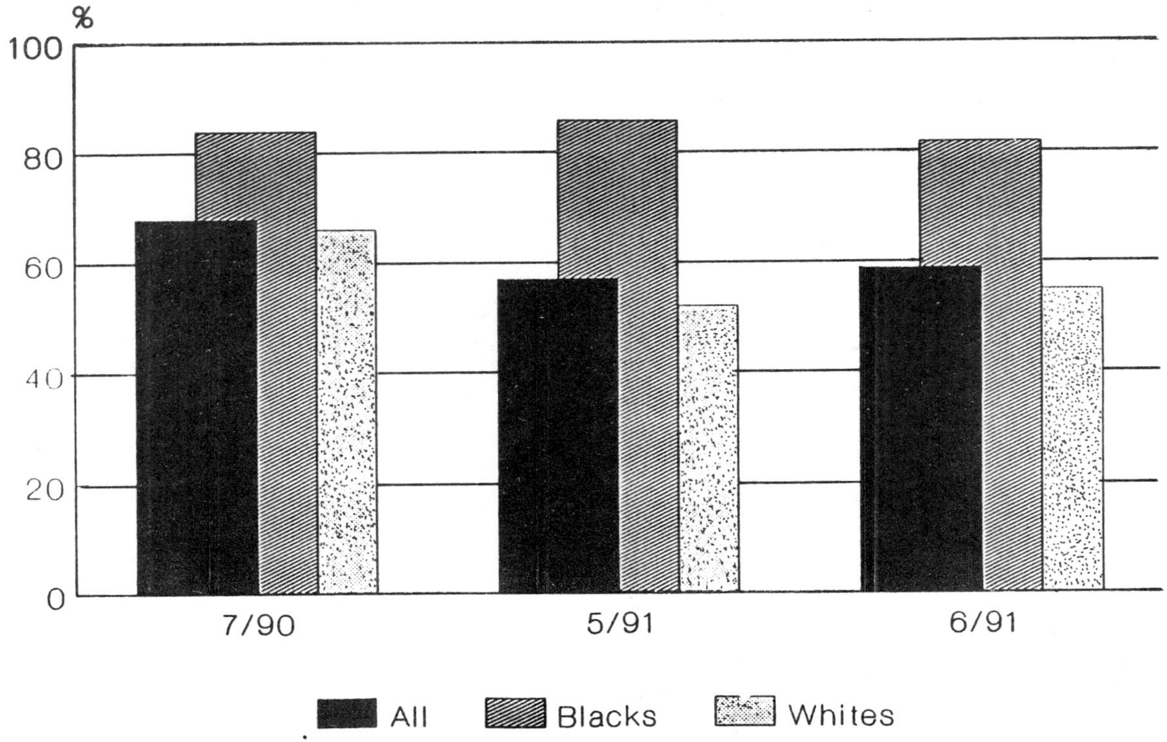

Source: The NBC News/Wall Street Journal Poll

Preferential Treatment for Women and Minorities

June 1991/December 1989

"Some people say that to make up for past discrimination, women and members of minority groups should be given preferential treatment in getting jobs and places in colleges. Others say that their ability, as determined in test scores, should be the main consideration. Which point of view comes closer to how you feel on the subject?"

	June 1991[1]	Dec. 1989[2]
Give preferential treatment	11 %	10 %
Test scores and abilities should be main consideration	81	84
Don't know	8	6

---

[1]*The Gallup Poll. (The results of the survey are based on personal interviews with a national sample of 990 adults, aged 18 and over, contacted during the period June 13-16, 1991—Error=4%.)*

[2]*The Gallup Poll. (The results of the survey are based on personal interviews with a national sample of 1,235 adults, aged 18 and over, contacted during the period December 7-10, 1989.)*

Fairness and Rationale for Racial Preference

June 1991/July 1988

"Do you think giving preference in hiring to blacks and other minorities takes jobs unfairly from whites, or not?"

	June 1991[1]
Yes	59 %
No	37
Don't know/No opinion	4

"Do you think blacks and other minorities should receive preference in college admissions to make up for past inequalities, or not?"

	June 1991[1]	July 1988[2]
Yes	22 %	18 %
No	76	76
Don't know	3	5

[1]*The ABC News/Washington Post Poll. (The results of the survey are based on telephone interviews with a sample of 1,511 adults, 18 and older, contacted within the continental United States during the period May 30–June 2, 1991.)*

[2]*Conducted by Media General/Associated Press. July 1988.*

Is Hiring Preference for Minorities Unfair to Whites?

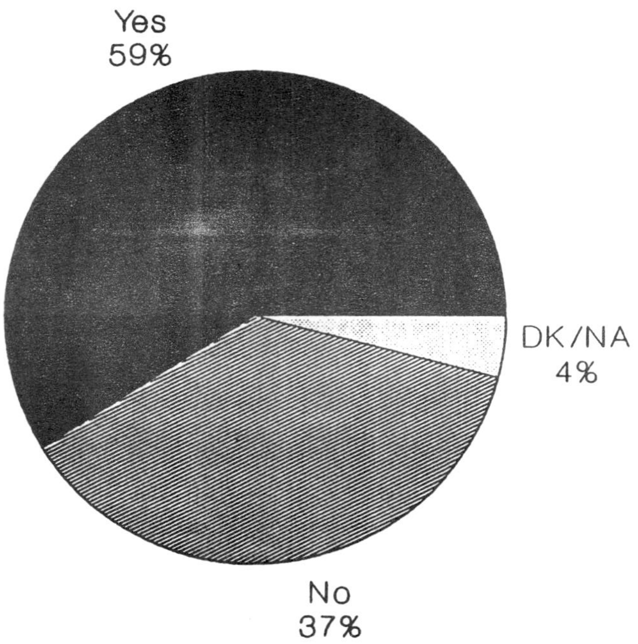

Source: The ABC News/Washington Post Poll, June 1991

Affirmative Action Statements

May 1991

"Let me read you some statements about affirmative action programs in education and employment. For each, tell me if you tend to agree or disagree (READ EACH STATEMENT)."

"After years of discrimination, it is only fair to set up special programs to make sure that women and minorities are given every chance to have equal opportunities in employment and education."

	Total	Blacks	Whites
Agree	79 %	96 %	76 %
Disagree	19	3	22
Not sure	2	1	2

"If there are no affirmative action programs helping women and minorities in employment and education, then these groups will continue to fail to get their share of jobs and higher education, thereby continuing past discrimination in the future."

	Total	Blacks	Whites
Agree	61 %	76 %	58 %
Disagree	36	23	39
Not sure	3	1	3

"As long as there are no rigid quotas, it makes sense to give special training and advice to women and minorities so that they can perform better on the job."

	Total	Blacks	Whites
Agree	78 %	85 %	77 %
Disagree	20	15	21
Not sure	2	-	2

continued on next page

"Minorities and women are not entitled to any special consideration."

	Total	Blacks	Whites
Agree	33 %	22 %	34 %
Disagree	66	76	64
Not sure	1	2	2

"Once affirmative action programs for women and minorities are started, the result is bound to be reverse discrimination against white men and imposition of a quota system."

	Total	Blacks	Whites
Agree	46 %	22 %	50 %
Disagree	48	75	45
Not sure	6	4	5

"White men learn faster, are better qualified and will continue to hold down the better jobs, no matter how many affirmative action programs for women and minorities are started."

	Total	Blacks	Whites
Agree	26 %	10 %	27 %
Disagree	72	86	70
Not sure	2	4	3

The Harris Survey. (The results of the survey are based on telephone interviews with a national sample of 1,256 adults, aged 18 and over, contacted during the period May 5-15, 1991.)

Have Affirmative Action Programs Helped Blacks?

May 1991

"Have affirmative-action programs helped blacks get better job opportunities?"

	Whites	Blacks
Helped	52 %	45 %
Hurt	10	5
No difference	28	41

Time/CNN Poll conducted by Yankelovich, Clancy & Shulman. (The results of the survey are based on telephone interviews with a national sample of 504 white and 504 black adults, 18 and older, contacted during the period May 24-29, 1991—Error=4.5%.)

Do Affirmative Action Programs Discriminate against Whites?

May 1991

"Do affirmative-action programs for blacks sometimes discriminate against whites? If 'yes', does this happen a lot or only sometimes?"

	Whites	Blacks
No	17 %	44 %
Yes	77	49
(Yes, a lot)	17	7
(Yes, sometimes)	60	42

Time/CNN Poll conducted by Yankelovich, Clancy & Shulman. (The results of the survey are based on telephone interviews with a national sample of 504 white and 504 black adults, 18 and older, contacted during the period May 24-29, 1991—Error=4.5%.)

Should Blacks Receive Preference over Equally Qualified Whites?

April 1991

"Do you believe that because of past discrimination against black people, qualified blacks should receive preference over equally qualified whites in such matters as getting into college or getting jobs?"

	Whites	Blacks
Should	18 %	48 %
Should not	72	42

Newsweek Poll conducted by The Gallup Organization. (The results of the survey are based on telephone interviews with a national sample of 305 blacks and 619 whites contacted during the period April 23-25 1991. "Don't Know" and other responses not shown.)

Fairness in Education without Quotas?

April 1991

"Can fairness in education, hiring and promotion be accomplished without quotas?"

	Whites	Blacks
Yes	59 %	26 %
No	29	61

Newsweek Poll conducted by The Gallup Organization. (The results of the survey are based on telephone interviews with a national sample of 305 blacks and 619 whites contacted during the period April 23-25, 1991. "Don't Know" and other responses not shown.)

Need for Affirmative Action Programs

March 1991

"Now let me read you two brief statements on affirmative action programs, and see which one comes closer to your point of view. STATEMENT A: Affirmative action programs are still needed to counteract the effects of discrimination against minorities, and are a good idea as long as there are no rigid quotas. STATEMENT B: Affirmative action programs have gone too far in favoring minorities, and should be phased out because they unfairly discriminate against whites. "Do you feel strongly about that, or not so strongly? (rotated)

Statement A/Strongly	40 %
Statement A/Not strongly	21
Statement B/Strongly	17
Statement B/Not strongly	11
Not sure	11

The NBC News/Wall Street Journal Poll. (The results of the survey are based on telephone interviews with a national sample of 1,505 registered voters, 18 and older, contacted during the period March 15-19, 1991.)

Are Affirmative Action Programs Still Needed?

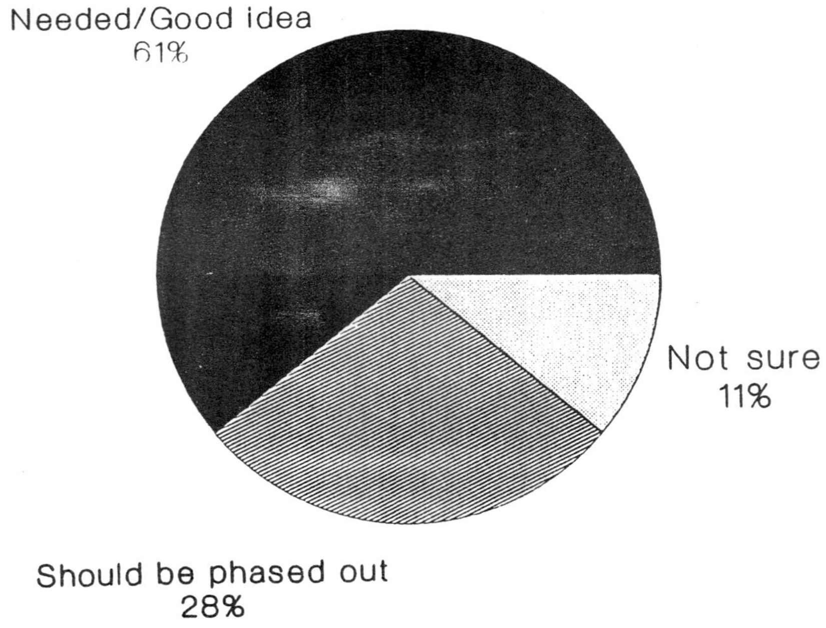

Source: The NBC News/Wall Street Journal Poll, March 1991

"Race-Norming"

March 1991

"Now I'd like to ask you a question on an employment practice. Here's an example of how it works. A White, a Black, and a Hispanic apply for a position as an auto mechanic and each get 300 correct answers on the same exam used to evaluate applicants. On the referral to the potential employer, the Black would be listed as scoring 83, the Hispanic 67 and the White 44 because the scores are altered based on race. But when the potential employer receives these scores, there is no mention of race. Therefore, it might appear that the Black applicant scored almost twice as high as the White applicant. Supporters of this practice say such a system is needed to compensate for tests that are biased against Blacks and Hispanics. Opponents say that altering test scores based on race can unfairly deny opportunity to those most qualified. From what you know, do you support or oppose this practice?"

Support	16 %
Oppose	77
Don't know	6

Conducted by Market Opinion Research. (The results of the sample are based on telephone interviews with a national sample of 580 registered voters contacted during the period March 19-24, 1991—Error not shown by the source.)

Reserving College Scholarships

January 1991

"Generally speaking, do you approve or disapprove of allowing colleges and universities to reserve some scholarships for minority students? (IF APPROVE OR DISAPPROVE) Is that (approve/disapprove) strongly or (approve/disapprove) somewhat?"

	All	Male	Female	Whites	Blacks	Latinos
Approve strongly	40 %	35 %	44 %	35 %	65 %	58 %
Approve somewhat	33	34	32	35	18	22
Disapprove somewhat	10	12	9	11	6	7
Disapprove strongly	14	17	11	16	7	11
Not sure	2	2	3	2	2	2
Refused	1	0	1	1	2	0

	Liberal	Middle	Conservative
Approve strongly	53 %	36 %	33 %
Approve somewhat	28	35	34
Disapprove somewhat	8	11	12
Disapprove strongly	10	14	18
Not sure	0	3	2
Refused	1	1	1

continued on next page

"Generally speaking, do you approve or disapprove of allowing colleges and universities to reserve some scholarships for white students? (IF APPROVE OR DISAPPROVE) Is that (approve/disapprove) strongly or (approve/disapprove) somewhat?"

	All	Male	Female	Whites	Blacks	Latinos
Approve strongly	36 %	30 %	40 %	34 %	45 %	36 %
Approve somewhat	31	33	30	32	27	27
Disapprove somewhat	14	15	13	14	9	17
Disapprove strongly	16	19	13	17	14	17
Not sure	2	2	3	2	3	3
Refused	1	1	1	1	2	0

	Liberal	Middle	Conservative
Approve strongly	43 %	33 %	32 %
Approve somewhat	28	34	31
Disapprove somewhat	13	14	15
Disapprove strongly	14	15	20
Not sure	1	3	1
Refused	1	1	1

The Los Angeles Times Poll. (The results are based on a telephone survey across the nation, including the states of Alaska and Hawaii, with a sample of 2,434 adults, 18 years of age or older, contacted during the period January 8-12, 1991.)

Fairness of Giving Preference to Blacks in Hiring or Promotion

December 1990

"When preference in hiring or promotion is given to blacks, do you think that it is fair to whites, or not fair to whites?"

Fair	24 %
Not fair	53
Depends	17
Don't know/No answer	6

The New York Times Poll. (The results of the survey are based on telephone interviews with a national sample of 1,028 adults, aged 18 and older, contacted during the period December 12-14, 1990.)

Preference in Hiring Or Promotion of Blacks Today?

December 1990/May 1990

"Do you believe that where there has been job discrimination against blacks in the past, preference in hiring or promotion should be given to blacks today?"

	December 1990[1]	May 1990[2]
Yes, preference	32 %	33 %
No	52	51
Depends	12	11
Don't know/No answer	4	5

[1]*The New York Times Poll. (The results of the survey are based on telephone interviews with a national sample of 1,028 adults, aged 18 and older, contacted during the period December 12-14, 1990.)*

[2]*The New York Times Poll. (The results of the survey are based on telephone interviews with a national sample of 1,140 adults, aged 18 and older, contacted during the period May 22-24, 1990.)*

Affirmative Action Programs without Rigid Quotas

January 1988

"Do you favor or oppose affirmative action programs for blacks and other minorities, which do not have rigid quotas?"

	Blacks	Whites
Favor	66 %	55 %
Oppose	18	24
Not sure	16	21

The BusinessWeek/Harris Poll. (The results of the survey are based on telephone interviews among national cross sections of 1,061 white adults and 531 black adults, 18 and older, contacted during the period January 20-26, 1988.)

2. Governmental Policies

The 1991 Civil Rights Bill

September 1991

"In June the U.S. House of Representatives passed a bill that would make it easier for blacks and women to bring lawsuits and collect damages in cases of job discrimination. The Bush Administration says the bill would lead employers to use quotas. But supporters of the bill say that would not happen because the bill would outlaw quotas. Do you favor this bill, or oppose this bill, or haven't you heard enough about it yet to have an opinion?"

	All	Whites	Blacks
Favor	11 %	10 %	21 %
Oppose	15	17	5
Haven't heard enough	71	70	70
Don't know/No answer	3	3	4

The New York Times Poll. (The results of the survey are based on telephone interviews with a national sample of 1,519 adults, aged 18 and older, contacted during the period September 3-5, 1991.)

Favor or Oppose the 1991 Civil Rights Bill?

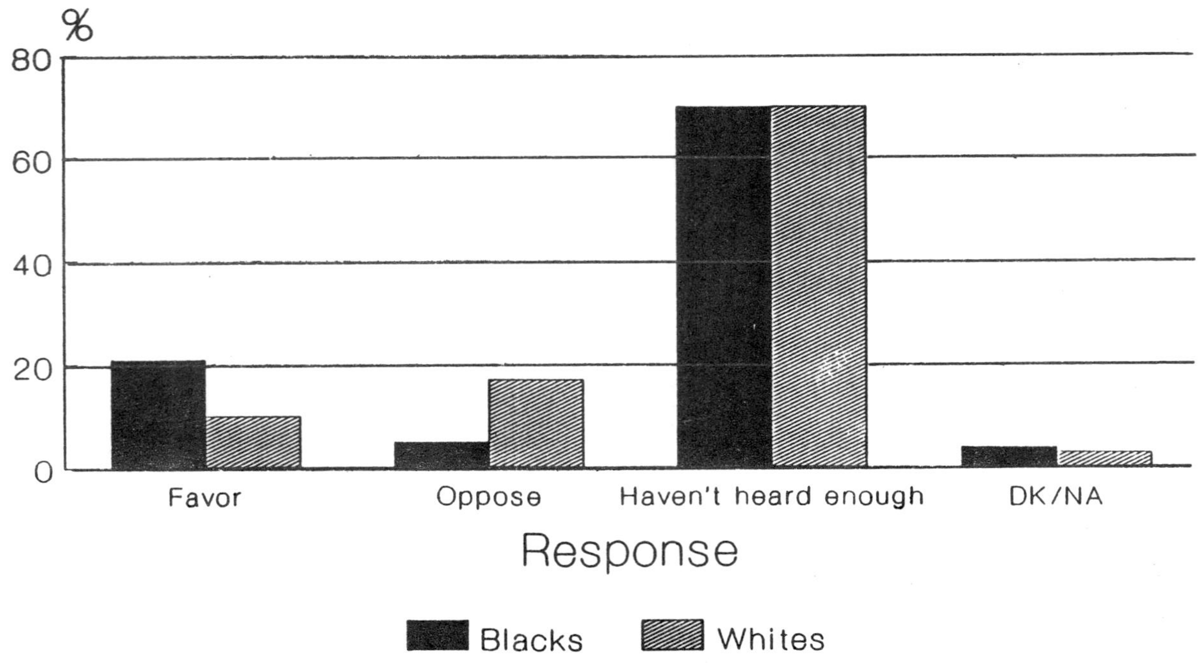

Source: The New York Times Poll,
September 1991

Laws Requiring Racial Preference

July 1991

"Do you favor or oppose federal laws requiring racial preference for minorities in employment and education, provided there are no rigid quotas?"

Favor	46 %
Oppose	48
Not sure	6

The Harris Survey. (The results of the survey are based on telephone interviews with a nationwide cross section of 1,250 adults, 18 and older, contacted during the period July 26-31, 1991.)

Laws Requiring Affirmative Action Programs

July 1991/June 1991/May 1991

"Do you favor or oppose federal laws requiring affirmative action programs for women and minorities in employment and education, provided there are no rigid quotas?"

	July 1991[1]	June 1991[2]	May 1991[3]
Favor	70 %	75 %	75 %
Oppose	24	22	22
Not sure	6	3	3

[1]*The Harris Survey. (The results of the survey are based on telephone interviews with a nationwide cross section of 1,250 adults, 18 and older, contacted during the period July 26-31, 1991.)*

[2]*The Harris Survey. (The results of the survey are based on interview with a national sample of 1,253 adults, aged 18 and over, contacted during the period June 20-24, 1991.)*

[3]*The Harris Survey. (The results of the survey are based on telephone interviews with a national sample of 1,256 adults, aged 18 and over, contacted during the period May 5-15, 1991.)*

Federal Government Actions to Help Blacks and Minorities

June 1991

"Which **one** of the following four actions by the federal government do you think would most help blacks and other minorities in our country? (rotated)"

Improving public education	46 %
Combating crime and drugs	22
Promoting growth in the economy	15
Ending job discrimination	15
Not sure	3

The NBC News/Wall Street Journal Poll. (The results are based on telephone interviews with a national sample of 1,006 registered voters contacted during the period June 22-25, 1991—Error=4%.)

Federal Government Actions That Would Help Minorities the Most

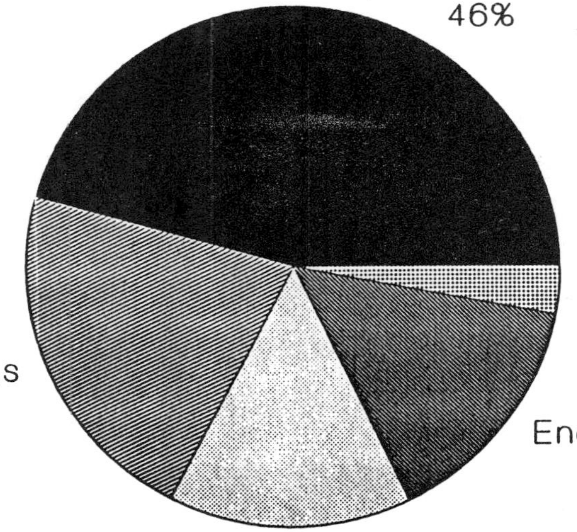

Source: The NBC News/Wall Street Journal Poll, June 1991

Does Congress Need to Legislate Against Discrimination?

June 1991

"Do you think the U.S. currently has enough federal laws and regulations aimed at reducing race, religion and sex discrimination, or does the Congress need to pass additional laws and regulations aimed at reducing this type of discrimination?"

	June 1991		
	All	Whites	Blacks
Enough federal laws	55 %	58 %	30 %
Need to pass additional laws	37	34	62
Don't know	8	8	8

The Gallup Poll. (The results of the survey are based on telephone interviews with a national sample of 990 adults, aged 18 and over, contacted during the period June 13-16, 1991—Error=4%.)

Options for Helping Blacks

June 1991

"Here are several ways people have suggested would help improve the situation of blacks in American society today. Do you favor or oppose each of these?"

	Favor	Oppose	Don't know
New laws requiring businesses to hire blacks in the same proportion as exists in the local community.	45 %	49 %	6 %
Spending more money to improve schools in black communities.	73	21	6
More Head Start programs to provide preschool education.	83	14	3
Spending more federal funds on job training programs.	72	24	4
Tougher federal laws with stiffer penalties for companies which discriminate in hiring and promoting.	64	29	7
Increasing federal assistance to blacks who want to start their own businesses	59	34	7

The Gallup Poll. (The results of the survey are based on telephone interviews with a national sample of 990 adults, 18 and older, contacted during the period June 13-16, 1991—Error=4%.)

Civil Rights Laws by Race

June 1991

"Do you think America's civil rights laws for [minorities, white men and people like yourself] go too far, not far enough or are they just about right]?"

	Go too far	Not far enough	Just about right	Don't know
Minorities	23 %	33 %	35 %	9 %
White men	14	17	62	7
People like yourself	2	39	54	5

The Los Angeles Times Poll. (The results of the survey are based on telephone interviews with a national sample of 1,439 adults, 18 and older, contacted during the period June 28-30, 1991.)

Political Battle Over the 1991 Civil Rights Bill

June 1991

"Have you seen, heard, or read anything about the civil rights bill now before Congress?"

	All	Whites	Blacks
Seen, heard or read	40 %	40 %	49 %
No have not	59	59	51
Don't know	1	1	-

"Congress is currently considering one civil rights bill sponsored by congressional Democrats, and another by the Bush Administration. Which of the two bills would you like to see Congress pass--or would you like to see neither bill pass?" (Asked only of those who have seen, heard or read about the bill--40% of the total sample)

	All	Whites	Blacks
Congressional Democrats	24 %	20 %	45 %
Bush Administration	25	28	8
Neither	27	27	25
Don't know	24	24	22

continued on next page

"Based on what you have heard or read about the two bills, which do you think requires racial quotas in hiring and promotion--the Democratic bill, the Bush Administration bill, neither, or both?" (Asked only of those who have seen, heard or read about the bill--40% of the total sample)

	All	Whites	Blacks
Democrats' bill	41 %	43 %	28 %
Bush Administration bill	10	11	8
Neither	20	18	32
Both do	10	9	17
Don't know	19	19	15

"Why do you think congressional Democrats are supporting new civil rights legislation at this time? Do you think it is [read each item]?" (Asked only of those who have seen, heard or read about the bill--40% of the total sample)

	All	Whites	Blacks
Mostly for partisan political advantage	61 %	65 %	30 %
Mostly because they feel new laws are needed to protect civil rights	32	29	54
Both	4	4	7
Neither	-	-	3
Don't know	3	2	6

"Why do you think President Bush has refused to support the Democratic version of the civil rights bill? Is it [read each item]?"

	All	Whites	Blacks
Mostly for partisan political advantage	28 %	27 %	34 %
Mostly because he feels the Democratic bill goes too far in encouraging racial quotas	61	63	50
Both	3	3	4
Neither	1	-	2
Don't know	7	7	10

The Gallup Poll. (The results of the survey are based on telephone interviews with a national sample of 990 adults, aged 18 and over, contacted during the period June 13-16, 1991—Error=4%.)

Opinions on Laws about Discrimination

June 1991/May 1991

"Thinking about civil rights laws designed to protect minorities from discrimination, which of the following statements comes closest to your point of view? (read from bottom on every other interview)"

	June 1991[1]			May 1991[2]		
	All	Whites	Blacks	All	Whites	Blacks
Current laws need to be toughened because they do not protect minorities well enough.	24 %	18 %	60 %	20 %	14 %	59 %
Current laws are right and protect minorities well enough.	23	26	10	34	37	11
Current laws have gone too far and have resulted in unfair quotas that cause reverse discrimination against people who do not qualify as minorities.	46	50	24	37	39	20
None of these	2	2	4	3	3	3
Not sure	3	4	2	6	7	7

[1]*The NBC News/Wall Street Journal Poll. (The results of the survey are based on telephone interviews with a national sample of 1,006 registered voters contacted during the period June 22-25, 1991—Error=4%.)*

[2]*The NBC News/Wall Street Journal Poll. (The results of the survey are based on telephone interviews with a national sample of 1,508 adults, 18 and older, contacted during the period May 10-14, 1991.)*

Attitudes Toward the 1991 Civil Rights Bill

June 1991/May 1991

"Have you seen or heard anything about the new civil rights bill currently before Congress? (IF YES, ASK:) Do you favor or oppose the civil rights bill?"

	June 1991[1]			May 1991[2]		
	All	Whites	Blacks	All	Whites	Blacks
Heard of Bill:						
Favor	12 %	10 %	26 %	8 %	7 %	18 %
Oppose	14	15	10	5	5	5
Not sure	9	10	8	5	5	7
Have not heard of bill	63	63	54	77	78	66
Not sure if heard of bill	2	2	2	5	5	4

"If this civil rights bill becomes law, do you think it will or will not affect your job or the job of someone in your household?"

	May 1991[2]		
	All	Whites	Blacks
Will	3 %	2 %	8 %
Will not	14	14	18
Not sure	1	1	4
Have not heard of it	82	83	70

"Do you know if President Bush favors or opposes this civil rights bill?" (Asked only of those who have heard of the bill--35% of the total sample)

	June 1991[1]		
	All	Whites	Blacks
Bush favors bill	3 %	3 %	4 %
Bush opposes bill	25	24	30
Not sure	7	6	9
Not asked	65	65	56

continued on next page

"Do you think he opposes the bill mainly because he believes it will help him politically, or mainly because he believes he is doing the right thing for the country?" (Asked only of those who know that Bush opposes the bill--25% of the total sample)

	June 1991[1]		
	All	Whites	Blacks
Will help him politically	30 %	26 %	53 %
Good for the country	63	67	35
Both	3	3	4
Neither	1	-	5
Not sure	2	2	4

[1]*The NBC News/Wall Street Journal Poll. (The results of the survey are based on telephone interviews with a national sample of 1,006 registered voters contacted during the period June 22-25, 1991—Error=4%.)*

[2]*The NBC News/Wall Street Journal Poll. (The results of the survey are based on telephone interviews with a national sample of 1,508 adults, 18 and older, contacted during the period May 10-14, 1991.)*

Need More Government Programs to Help Blacks?

May 1991

"Do we need more government efforts to help blacks get better job opportunities, are existing programs adequate, or do they go too far?"

	Whites	Blacks
More programs	19 %	58 %
Adequate	41	23
Go too far	31	13

Time/CNN Poll conducted by Yankelovich Clancy Shulman. (The results of the survey are based on telephone interviews with a national sample of 504 white and 504 black adults, 18 and older, contacted during the period May 24-29, 1991—Error=4.5%.)

Enough Legislation to Improve Conditions of Blacks?

April 1991

"Is there enough legislation on the books to improve conditions for blacks in this country, with further progress coming through private efforts? Or is more legislation needed?

	Whites	Blacks
Enough legislation	53 %	24 %
More legislation needed	35	64

Newsweek Poll conducted by The Gallup Organization. (The results of the survey are based on telephone interviews with a national sample of 305 blacks and 619 whites contacted during the period April 23-25 1991. "Don't Know" and other responses not shown.)

Should Bush Have Vetoed or Signed 1990 Civil Rights Bill?

October 1990

"Congress recently passed a civil rights bill it said would increase job rights for minority groups and women. George Bush vetoed the bill saying it would have required quotas. Do you think George Bush should have vetoed that bill or should he have signed it into law?"

Vetoed	40 %
Signed	47
Don't know/No answer	14

The New York Times Poll. (The results of the survey are based on telephone interviews with a national sample of 1,445 adults, aged 18 and older, contacted during the period October 28-31, 1990.)

Should Census Figures be Adjusted to Count for Missed Groups?

March 1990

"It has been suggested that parts of certain groups in America, particularly minorities and the poor in inner cities, are missed and not counted by the census. The suggestion has been made that the government estimate how many people are missed, and add these estimates into the final census count. Other people say that the census should only include the actual number of people counted. Which of these views comes closer to your own?"

Include estimates in counts	48 %
Only include actual number counted	45
Don't know	7

The Gallup Poll. (The results of the survey are based on telephone interviews with a national sample of 1,225 adults, aged 18 and over, contacted during the period March 15-18, 1990.)

More Government Spending and Taxes for Enterprise Zones in Ghettos?

February 1989

"If you had to choose, would you favor more government spending on creating enterprise zones in black ghetto areas even if it means raising taxes, or would you favor no more federal spending on creating enterprise zones in black ghetto areas and not raising taxes?

Favor federal spending with more tax	42 %
No more federal spending, no tax raise	50
Not sure	8

The Harris Survey. (The results of the survey are based on telephone interviews with a national sample of 1,250 adults, aged 18 and over, contacted during the period February 10-14, 1989.)

C. OTHER ATTITUDES REGARDING DISCRIMINATION

Racial Treatment -- Special, Fair or Discriminatory?

May 1991/July 1990

"For each of the following groups, please tell me if you feel they are receiving too many special advantages, receiving fair treatment, or if they are being discriminated against. (read and rotated)"

Hispanics

	May 1991[1]			July 1990[2]		
	All	Whites	Blacks	All	Whites	Blacks
Special advantages	12 %	13 %	10 %	11 %	10 %	15 %
Fair treatment	48	50	26	47	51	29
Discriminated against	27	23	52	27	24	47
Not sure	13	14	12	15	16	9

Blacks

	May 1991			July 1990		
	All	Whites	Blacks	All	Whites	Blacks
Special advantages	17 %	20 %	2 %	14 %	15 %	1 %
Fair treatment	45	48	22	43	47	20
Discriminated against	32	26	70	36	29	76
Not sure	6	6	6	7	8	3

Asian-Americans

	May 1991			July 1990		
	All	Whites	Blacks	All	Whites	Blacks
Special advantages	12 %	12 %	19 %	14 %	12 %	28 %
Fair treatment	54	57	36	48	51	32
Discriminated against	17	14	29	21	19	28
Not sure	17	17	16	17	18	12

[1]*The NBC/Wall Street Journal Poll. (The results of the survey are based on telephone interviews with a national sample of 1,508 adults, 18 and older, contacted during the period May 10-14, 1991.)*

[2]*The NBC/Wall Street Journal Poll. (The results of the survey are based on telephone interviews with a national sample of 1,555 registered voters, 18 and older, contacted during the period July 6-10, 1990.)*

Are Police Tougher on Blacks?

April 1991

"Do you think the police in most big cities are generally tougher on whites than on blacks, or tougher on blacks than on whites, or do the police treat them both the same?

Tougher on whites	— %
Tougher on blacks	51
Treat the same	34
Don't know/no answer	15

"What about the police in your community? Do you think the police in your community are generally tougher on whites than on blacks, or tougher on blacks than on whites, or do the police treat them both the same?"

Tougher on whites	1 %
Tougher on blacks	19
Treat the same	66
Don't know/no answer	14

The CBS News/New York Times Poll. (The results of the survey are based on telephone interviews with a national sample of 1,283 adults, 18 and older, contacted during the period April 1-3, 1991.)

Perceived Rate of Police Brutality against Minorities

March 1991

"How much police brutality against members of minority groups do you think there is around the country these days?"

A lot	21 %
Considerable	41
Little	21
Very Little	10

The Newsweek Poll. (The results of the survey are based on telephone interviews of a national sample contacted during the period March 14-15, 1991.)

Government Investigation of Black Elected Officials

June 1990

"Some people say the government deliberately singles out and investigates black elected officials in order to discredit them in a way it doesn't do with white officials. Do you think that is true, or that it might possibly be true, or that it is almost certainly not true?"

	All	White	Black
True	13 %	6 %	32 %
Might possibly be true	34	28	45
Almost certainly not true	43	57	16
Don't know/No answer	10	9	7

The CBS News/New York Times Poll. (The results of the survey are based on telephone interviews with a national sample of 1,047 adults, 18 and older, contacted during the period June 17-20, 1990.)

Agree with Discrimination by Private Clubs?

February 1989

"Private membership clubs primarily devoted to business should have the right to deny membership to anyone based on race, religion or sex."

Agree	20 %
Disagree	75
Not sure	5

American Civil Liberties Union Poll conducted by Peter D. Hart Research Associates. (The results of the survey are based on telephone interviews with a national sample of 1,003 adults, 18 and older, contacted during the period February 21-25, 1989—Error not shown in source.)

Discrimination by Private Clubs

July 1988

"Do you think that private clubs should or should not have the right to exclude prospective members on the basis of their Sex? Race? Religion? Nationality?"

	Should	Should not	No opinion
Sex	37 %	56 %	7 %
Race	18	78	4
Religion	17	80	3
Nationality	17	80	3

The Gallup Poll. (The results of the survey are based on telephone interviews with a national sample of 1,000 adults, aged 18 and over, contacted during the period July 1-7, 1988—Error=4%.)

IV. RACE AND GOVERNMENTAL INSTITUTIONS

A. THE FEDERAL GOVERNMENT

Government Help for Blacks

March 1992

"I am going to read you a few statements and for each I'd like you to tell me whether you tend to agree or disagree with it, or if perhaps you have no opinion about the statement: Because of past discrimination, blacks who need it should get some help from the government that white people in similar economic circumstances don't get."

	Whites	Blacks
Agree	21 %	41 %
Disagree	57	41
Don't know	22	18

The Washington Post Poll conducted by ICR Research Services. (The results of the survey are based on telephone interviews with a national sample of 914 whites and 414 blacks, aged 18 and over, contacted during the period February 28-March 3, 1992.)

Should Government Make Efforts to Help Minorities?

May 1991

"Which of the following statements comes closer to your point of view: The federal government should make special efforts to improve the social and economic position of blacks and other minority groups to correct past discrimination, OR, The federal government should not make any special efforts to improve the social and economic position of blacks and other minorities, because they should help themselves. (rotated)"

	All	Whites	Blacks
Should make special efforts	45 %	39 %	82 %
Should not make special efforts	41	46	11
Somewhere in between (volunteered)	10	10	6
Neither (volunteered)	1	2	-
Not sure	3	3	1

The NBC News/Wall Street Journal Poll. (The results of the survey are based on telephone interviews with a national sample of 1,508 adults, 18 and older, contacted during the period May 10-14, 1991.)

Should the Federal Government Make Special Efforts to Help Minorities?

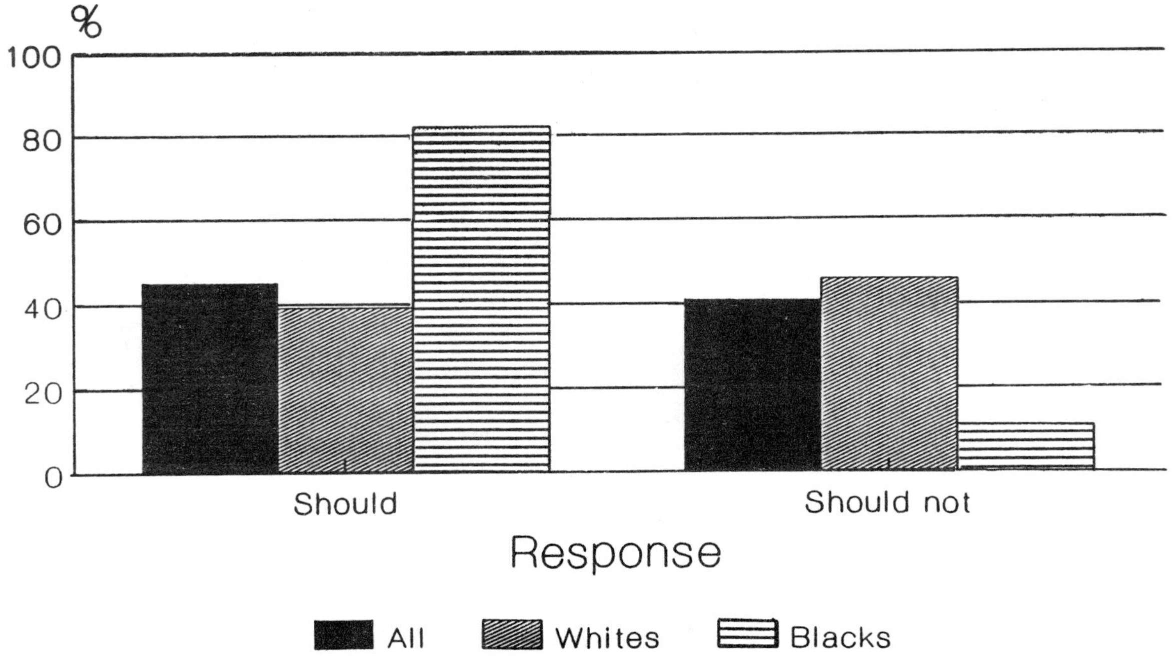

Source: The NBC News/Wall Street Journal Poll, May 1991

Federal Government Paying Too Much Attention to Problems of Minorities?

December 1990/December 1989

"Do you think the government in Washington has been paying too much attention to the problems of minorities, or about the right amount, or do you think they haven't been paying enough attention to the problems of minorities?"

	December 1990[1]					December 1989[2]
	All	East	Midwest	South	West	All
Too much	22 %	19 %	23 %	25 %	21 %	20 %
Right	33	30	34	34	36	35
Not enough	38	43	36	36	37	39
Not sure	6	8	6	5	5	5
Refused	1	0	1	0	1	1

[1]*The Los Angeles Times Poll. (The results are based on a telephone survey across the nation, including the states of Alaska and Hawaii, with a sample of 2,200 adults, 18 years of age or older, contacted during the period December 8-12, 1990.)*

[2]*The Los Angeles Times Poll. (The results are based on a telephone survey across the nation, including the states of Alaska and Hawaii, with a sample of 2,095 adults, 18 years of age or older, contacted during the period December 16-20, 1989.)*

Less was Done by the Government for Minorities in the Past Decade?

June 1990

"Now let me read you some things that some people say were among the important things that happened over the past 10 years. For each, tell me if you feel that was something that was positive or negative for the country...Less was done by the government for minorities, leaving them more on their own"

Positive	38 %
Negative	59
Not sure	3

The Harris Survey. (The results of the survey are based on telephone interviews with a national sample of 1,254 adults, aged 18 and over, contacted during the period June 21-26, 1990.)

Should Government Do More to Help Blacks?

May 1990/January 1988

"Do you think the government should do more to help blacks, or has it done enough, or has it done too much already?"

	May 1990[1]	January 1988[2]
Do more	33 %	35 %
Done enough	43	45
Done too much	15	11
Don't know/No answer	9	9

[1]*The CBS News/New York Times Poll. (The results of the survey are based on telephone interviews with a national sample of 1,140 adults, aged 18 and older, contacted during the period May 22-24, 1990.)*

[2]*The CBS News/New York Times Poll. (The results of the survey are based on telephone interviews with a national sample of 1,663 adults, 18 and older, contacted during the period January 17-21, 1988. Wording note: "Do you think the government should do more to help blacks, or has it done enough already, or has it done too much already?")*

Active Government Role Sought for Minorities?

November 1989

"If you had to say, would you like to see the federal government more active or less active... In moving faster toward ending discrimination against minorities, such as blacks and Hispanics?"

More active	73 %
Less active	19
No change (volunteered)	6
Not sure	2

The Harris Survey. (The results of the survey are based on telephone interviews with a national sample of 1,249 adults, aged 18 and over, contacted during the period October27-November 1, 1989.)

The Agenda for the Federal Government -- Blacks

November 1988

"During the next four years, do you want the federal government... to pay more attention, less attention, or the same amount of attention to the concerns of blacks?"

More	46 %
Less	7
Same	39
Don't know/No answer	8

The New York Times Poll. (The results of the survey are based on telephone interviews with a national sample of 1,627 adults, aged 18 and older, contacted during the period November 10-16, 1988.)

The Government Pays Too Much Attention to Blacks?

October/May 1988

"Do you think the United States government is paying too much attention, too little attention, or about the right amount of attention to the needs of blacks?" (Asked only of registered voters—76% of the total sample)

	October 1988[1]	May 1988[2]
Too much	14 %	17 %
Too little	36	34
Right amount	41	41
Don't Know/No Answer	9	8

[1]*The CBS News/New York Times Poll. (The results of the survey are based on telephone interviews with a national sample of 1,827 adults, aged 18 and older, contacted during the period October 21-24, 1988.)*

[2]*The CBS News/New York Times Poll. (The results of the survey are based on telephone interviews with a national sample of 1,382 registered voters, contacted during the period May 9-12, 1988.)*

Government Pays Too Much Attention to Blacks and Minorities?

July 1988

"Do you think the government pays to much attention to blacks and other minorities, or the right amount, or do you think the government pays too little attention to blacks and other minorities?"

Too much attention	30 %
Right amount of attention	34
Too little attention	27
Not sure	8
Refused	1

The Los Angeles Times Poll. (The results are based on a telephone survey across the nation, including the states of Alaska and Hawaii, with a sample of 2,277 adults, 18 years of age or older, contacted during the period July 5-10, 1988.)

B. THE PRESIDENT

Approval of President Bush's Handling of Civil Rights

June 1991

"Do you approve or disapprove of the way Bush is handling civil rights?"

Approve	62 %
Disapprove	28
Don't know/No opinion	11

The ABC News/Washington Post Poll. (The results of the survey are based on telephone interviews with a sample of 1,511 adults, 18 and older, contacted within the continental United States during the period May 30-June 2, 1991.)

Approval of President Bush's Handling of Race Relations

June 1991/March 1991/January 1991/May 1990

"Do you approve or disapprove of the way Bush is handling race relations?"

	6/91[1]	3/91[2]	1/91[3]	5/90[4]
Approve	60 %	68 %	63 %	65 %
Disapprove	27	22	24	29
Don't know/No opinion	13	10	13	6

[1]*The ABC News/Washington Post Poll. (The results of the survey are based on telephone interviews with a sample of 1,511 adults, 18 and older, contacted within the continental United States during the period May 30-June 2, 1991.)*

[2]*The ABC News/Washington Post Poll. (The results of the survey are based on telephone interviews with a sample of 1,215 adults, 18 and older, contacted within the continental United States during the period March 1-4, 1991.)*

[3]*The ABC News/Washington Post Poll. (The results of the survey are based on telephone interviews with a sample of 1,015 adults, 18 and older, contacted within the continental United States during the period January 23-27, 1991.)*

[4]*The ABC News/Washington Post Poll. May 21, 1990.*

President Bush and Domestic Programs -- Race Problems

March 1991

"Now let me ask you about some specific problems facing the country. As I read off each one, would you tell me whether you approve or disapprove of the way President Bush is handling that problem... Handling race relations?"

Approve	63 %
Disapprove	26
Don't know	11

The Gallup Poll. (The results of the survey are based on telephone interviews with a national sample of 1,018 adults, aged 18 and over, contacted during the period March 7-10, 1991—Error=4%.)

President Bush's Handling of National Issues -- Minorities and Poor

March 1991/November 1990

"Here is a list of some problems and responsibilities facing the president and his administration. Do you think George Bush is making progress or is not making progress on handling each of these different problems? -- Improving the lot of minorities and the poor"

	March 1991[1]	November 1991[2]
Progress	38 %	28 %
No progress	53	62
Don't know	9	10

[1]*The Gallup Poll. (The results of the survey are based on telephone interviews with a national sample of 1,018 adults, aged 18 and over, contacted during the period March 7-10, 1991—Error=4%.)*

[2]*The Gallup Poll. (The results of the survey are based on telephone interviews with a national sample of 1,008 adults, aged 18 and over, contacted during the period November 8-11, 1990. Varied Wording: "Here is a list of some problems and responsibilities facing the president and his Administration. After nearly two years in office, do you think George Bush is making progress or is not making progress on handling each of these different problems? -- Improving the lot of minorities and the poor")*

President Bush's Report Card for Civil Rights

January 1991

"And, what kind of report card would you give President Bush in handling civil rights in this country? You can give him an A plus all the way down to a D minus, or you can give him an F for failure."

	Total	Male	Female	Whites	Blacks	Latinos
A+	2 %	2 %	1 %	1 %	1 %	2 %
A	8	9	8	9	3	10
A-	1	1	1	1	1	1
B+	3	3	2	3	2	2
B	25	27	23	27	10	17
B-	3	3	3	3	1	1
C+	3	4	2	3	3	2
C	27	27	27	28	23	23
C-	3	4	3	3	5	4
D+	0	0	1	0	1	0
D	9	7	10	8	15	14
D-	2	1	2	2	6	2
F	6	6	7	4	24	9
Not sure	8	6	9	8	5	12
Refused	0	0	1	0	0	1

	Liberal	Middle	Conservative
A+	1 %	1 %	2 %
A	6	7	11
A-	0	0	2
B+	1	3	4
B	19	25	30
B-	2	2	4
C+	4	3	3
C	26	31	24
C-	5	4	2
D+	1	0	0
D	14	9	5
D-	3	1	1
F	12	5	5
Not sure	6	9	7
Refused	0	0	0

The Los Angeles Times Poll. (The results are based on a telephone survey across the nation, including the states of Alaska and Hawaii, with a sample of 2,434 adults, 18 years of age or older, contacted during the period January 8-12, 1991.)

The Bush Administration and Problems of Minorities

January 1991

"Do you think the Bush administration has been paying too much attention to the problems of minorities, or about the right amount, or do you think they haven't been paying enough attention to the problems of minorities?"

	All	Male	Female	Whites	Blacks	Latinos
Too much	7 %	6 %	8 %	8 %	2 %	2 %
Right amount	42	47	38	47	13	27
Not enough	43	41	45	37	81	61
Not sure	7	5	8	7	4	7
Refused	1	1	1	1	0	3

	Liberal	Middle	Conservative
Too much	5 %	7 %	8 %
Right amount	34	43	53
Not enough	58	40	32
Not sure	3	8	6
Refused	0	2	1

The Los Angeles Times Poll. (The results are based on a telephone survey across the nation, including the states of Alaska and Hawaii, with a sample of 2,434 adults, 18 years of age or older, contacted during the period January 8-12, 1991.)

Does President Bush Care about Black People?

January 1990

"How much do you think George Bush cares about the needs and problems of black people--a great deal, some, or not much?"

Great deal	20 %
Some	49
Not much	24
Don't know/No answer	7

The CBS News/New York Times Poll. (The results of the survey are based on telephone interviews with a national sample of 1,557 adults, 18 and older, contacted during the period January 13-15, 1990.)

President Bush's Handling of Civil Rights

December 1989

"Now I'd like to ask some questions about civil rights in this country. First, do you approve of the job President Bush is doing to protect the civil rights of individuals?"

Approve of Bush's job on civil rights	62 %
Disapprove of Bush's job on civil rights	23
Don't know	15

The Gallup Poll. (The results of the survey are based on personal interviews with a national sample of 1,235 adults, aged 18 and over, contacted during the period December 7-10, 1989.)

President Bush's Ratings on Helping Minorities and the Poor

February 1989

"Now let me ask you specifics about President Bush. How would you rate him on wanting to help the poor and minorities, excellent, pretty good, only fair, or poor?"

Excellent	22 %
Pretty good	33
Only fair	28
Poor	14
Not sure	3

The Harris Survey. (The results of the survey are based on telephone interviews with a national sample of 1,250 adults, contacted during the period February 10-14, 1989.

Is President Bush Sensitive to Minorities?

August 1988

"Do you think George Bush is sensitive to the feelings of minorities?" (Asked only of registered voters--76% of the total sample)

Yes	45 %
No	34
Don't know/No answer	21

The CBS News/New York Times Poll. The results of the survey are based on telephone interviews with a national sample of 1,689 adults, 18 and older, contacted during the period August 19-21, 1988.

C. CONGRESS AND THE POLITICAL PARTIES

Party That Can Best Deal with Race Relations

November 1991

"Which political party, the Republican or the Democratic, do you think would do a better job of dealing with each of the following... Race relations?"

Democratic	53 %
Republican	29
No Difference/No Opinion	18

The Gallup Poll. (The results of the survey are based on telephone interviews with a national sample of 1,219 adults, aged 18 and over, contacted during the period October 31-November 3, 1991.)

Approval of Congress' Handling of Civil Rights

June 1991

"Do you approve or disapprove of the way Congress is handling civil rights?"

Approve	53 %
Disapprove	33
Don't know/No opinion	13

The ABC News/Washington Post Poll. (The results of the survey are based on telephone interviews with a sample of 1,511 adults, 18 and older, contacted within the continental United States during the period May 30-June 2, 1991.)

Which Party Represents Minority Interests Better?

June 1991

"Which political party do you think does a better job representing the interests of blacks and other minorities -- the Democrats or the Republicans?"

Democrats	56 %
Republicans	21
Neither (volunteered)	5
Equal (volunteered)	5
Don't know/No opinion	13

The ABC News/Washington Post Poll. (The results of the survey are based on telephone interviews with a sample of 1,511 adults, 18 and older, contacted within the continental United States during the period May 30-June 2, 1991.)

Which Party Represents Your Civil Rights Views?

June 1991

"Which party, the Democrats or the Republicans, generally comes closest to reflecting your views on civil rights?"

Democrats	46 %
Republicans	35
Neither (volunteered)	5
Equal (volunteered)	3
Don't know/No opinion	12

The ABC News/Washington Post Poll. (The results of the survey are based on telephone interviews with a sample of 1,511 adults, 18 and older, contacted within the continental United States during the period May 30-June 2, 1991.)

Political Party that Represents Your Civil Rights Views

June 1991

"Which political party best represents your views on civil rights for blacks and other minorities -- the Republican Party or the Democratic Party? (rotated)"

	All	Whites	Blacks
Republicans	33 %	37 %	6 %
Democrats	48	42	85
Both (volunteered)	3	3	3
Neither (volunteered)	7	7	2
Not sure	10	11	4

The NBC News/Wall Street Journal Poll. (The results are based on telephone interviews with a national sample of 1,006 registered voters contacted during the period June 22-25, 1991—Error=4%.)

Political Parties' Ratings on Policies Designed to Reduce Discrimination

June 1991

"As far as you know, does the Democratic Party favor or oppose racial quotas?" (rotated with next question)

Democrats favor quotas	50 %
Democrats oppose quotas	14
Not sure	36

"As far as you know, does the Republican Party favor or oppose racial quotas?" (rotated with previous question)

Republicans favor quotas	18 %
Republicans oppose quotas	47
Not sure	36

"Do you think the Republican Party favors or opposes hiring preference for blacks and other minorities to make up for past discrimination against them? (rotated with next question)

	All	Whites	Blacks
Republicans favor hiring preference	18 %	18 %	13 %
Republicans oppose hiring preference	57	54	74
Not sure	26	28	13

"Do you think the Democratic Party favors or opposes hiring preference for blacks and other minorities to make up for past discrimination against them?" (rotated with previous question)

	All	Whites	Blacks
Democrats favor hiring preference	53 %	52 %	60 %
Democrats oppose hiring preference	20	19	21
Not sure	28	30	19

continued on next page

"Do you think the Republican Party favors or opposes affirmative action programs in business for blacks and other minority groups?" (rotated with next question)

	All	Whites	Blacks
Republicans favor affirmative action	34 %	37 %	15 %
Republicans oppose affirmative action	42	38	71
Not sure	24	26	15

"Do you think the Democratic Party favors or opposes affirmative action programs in business for blacks and other minority groups?" (rotated with previous question)

	All	Whites	Blacks
Democrats favor affirmative action	71 %	69 %	83 %
Democrats oppose affirmative action	8	7	9
Not sure	21	23	8

The NBC News/Wall Street Journal Poll. (The results are based on telephone interviews with a national sample of 1,006 registered voters contacted during the period June 22-25, 1991—Error=4%.)

Which Party Cares More About the Problems of Blacks/Whites?

June 1991/April 1990

"Who do you think cares more about the needs and problems of blacks--the Republican party or the Democratic party?"

	June 1991[1]	April 1990[2]
Republican party	15 %	13 %
Democratic party	56	55
Both (volunteered)	8	8
Neither (volunteered)	5	5
Don't know/No answer	17	19

"Who do you think cares more about the needs and problems of whites, the Republican party or the Democratic party?"

	June 1991[1]
Republican party	45 %
Democratic party	19
Both (volunteered)	14
Neither (volunteered)	5
Don't know/No answer	17

[1]*The CBS News/New York Times Poll. (The results of the survey are based on telephone interviews with a national sample of 1,424 adults, aged 18 and older, contacted during the period June 3-6, 1991.)*

[2]*The CBS News/New York Times Poll. (The results of the survey are based on telephone interviews with a national sample of 1,515 adults, aged 18 and older, contacted during the period March 30-April 2, 1990.)*

Political Party That Best Represents Your Civil Rights Views

October 1988

"Which political party -- the Democrats or the Republicans -- do you think best represents your views on civil rights?"

The Democrats	48 %
The Republicans	34
Not sure	18

The NBC News/Wall Street Journal Poll. (The results of the survey are based on telephone interviews with a national sample of 1,285 voters, 18 and older, contacted during the period October 23-26, 1988.)

D. THE SUPREME COURT

Important to Have a Black Person on the Supreme Court?

September 1991

"Do you think it is important or not important that there always be at least one black person on the Supreme Court?"

	Total	Whites	Blacks
Important	50 %	46 %	75 %
Not important	47	51	23
Don't know/No answer	3	3	2

The CBS News/New York Times Poll. (The results of the survey are based on telephone interviews with a national sample of 1,519 adults, aged 18 and older, contacted during the period September 3-5, 1991.)

Approval of Supreme Court Rulings -- Racial Issues

July 1991

"Please tell me whether you generally approve or disapprove of the Supreme Court's rulings over the past years in each of the following areas. First do you approve or disapprove of its rulings in cases where racial discrimination, affirmative action or racial quotas are an issue?"

Approve	39 %
Disapprove	37
Don't know	24

The Gallup Poll. (The results of the survey are based on telephone interviews with a national sample of 1,217 adults, 18 and older, contacted during the period July 11-14, 1991.)

E. THE ELECTORAL PROCESS

Race as an Issue in the 1992 Presidential Campaign

November 1991

"As I read a list of issues, please tell me whether each is important or not important in determining which presidential candidate you will vote for in next year's elections... Race relations." (Asked only of registered voters -- 81% of the total sample)

Yes	70 %
No	28
Don't Know	2

The Gallup Poll. (The results of the survey are based on telephone interviews with a national sample of 1,219 adults, aged 18 and over, contacted during the period October 31-November 3, 1991.)

Political Fallout from President Bush's Veto of Civil Rights Bill

June 1991

"President Bush and the Democratic Congress have had major disagreements over bills the Congress has passed. As a result, he has vetoed or has threatened to veto many key bills. Let me read you several bills where that has happened. (The Civil Rights Act of 1991) Do you think President Bush is more right or more wrong to veto that bill?"

More right	36 %
More wrong	38
Not sure	26

"If you had to vote for President Bush in 1992 just on the basis of that veto, would you vote for or against him? -- The Civil Rights Act of 1991"

	Total Sample	"More Right" Respondents*	"More Wrong" Respondents**
Vote for Bush	56 %	89 %	17 %
Vote against Bush	40	8	78
Not sure	4	3	5

The Harris Survey. (The results of the survey are based on telephone interviews with a national sample of 1,253 adults, 18 and older, contacted during the period June 20-24, 1991.)

*"More Right" respondents constitute 36% of the total sample.

**"More Wrong" respondents constitute 38% of the total sample.

The Democratic Candidate and the Quota Issue

June 1991

"Suppose that you, yourself, were able to select the Democratic Party's candidate for president in 1992. Which of the following would be important considerations in selecting the candidate? -- The candidate's views on whether women and minorities can be protected from job discrimination without the use of quotas in hiring and promotion (Based on Democrats and Democratic leaners.)"

All	85 %
Liberals	86
Conservatives	85

"When choosing a Democratic presidential candidate would you prefer?" (Respondents who rated an issue as important in previous question were asked which position on the issue they preferred. Based on Democrats and Democratic leaners.)

	All	Liberals	Conservatives
Oppose quotas in hiring and promotion as a form of reverse discrimination	40 %	40 %	38 %
Favor quotas in hiring and promotion as necessary to protect women and minorities	40	39	43

The Gallup Poll. (The results of the survey are based on telephone interviews with a national sample of 1,000 adults, 18 and older, contacted during the period June 27-30, 1991—Error=6%.)

Preference for President

December 1989/July 1988

"Now, I'd like to read you the descriptions of two imaginary men—call them Mr. A and Mr. B. Suppose for a moment that both are running for president of the United States and you have to vote for one of them. Here are their descriptions: Mr. A is about 55 years old, he was born in Portland Oregon, he is black, he is married with two children and is a businessman. Mr. B is about 60 years old, he was born and raised in Cleveland, Ohio, he is married with one child and his career has been as an attorney. Which man would you vote for, Mr. A or Mr. B?"

	Dec. 1989[1]	July 1988[2]
Mr. A	37 %	29 %
Mr. B	43	46
Not sure	18	18
Refused	2	7

"Now, I'd like to read you the descriptions of two imaginary men—call them Mr. A and Mr. B. Suppose for a moment that both are running for president of the United States and you have to vote for one of them. Here are their descriptions: Mr. A is about 55 years old, he was born and raised in Portland, Oregon, he is married with two children and is a businessman. Mr. B is about 60 years old, he was born and raised in Cleveland, Ohio, he is black, is married with one child and his career has been as an attorney. Which man would you vote for, Mr. A or Mr. B?"

	Dec. 1989[3]	July 1988[4]
Mr. A	46 %	46 %
Mr. B	33	37
Not sure	19	12
Refused	2	5

[1]*The Los Angeles Times Poll. (The results are based on a telephone survey across the nation, including the states of Alaska and Hawaii, with a sample of 2,095 adults, 18 years of age or older, contacted during the period December 16-20, 1989. Question was asked only of respondents whose telephone numbers end in 1, 3. 5, or 7: Original Print source does not show the percentage of these respondents with respect to the total sample.)*

[2]*The Los Angeles Times Poll. (The results are based on a telephone survey across the nation, including the states of Alaska and Hawaii, with a sample of 2,277 adults, 18 years of age or older, contacted during the period July 5-10, 1988. Question was asked only of respondents whose telephone numbers end in 2, 4, 6, or 8: Original Print source does not show the percentage of these respondents with respect to the total sample.)*

continued on next page

[3]*The Los Angeles Times Poll. (The results are based on a telephone survey across the nation, including the states of Alaska and Hawaii, with a sample of 2,095 adults, 18 years of age or older, contacted during the period December 16-20, 1989. Question was asked only of respondents whose telephone numbers end in 2, 4. 6, or 8: Original Print source does not show the percentage of these respondents with respect to the total sample.)*

[4]*The Los Angeles Times Poll. (The results are based on a telephone survey across the nation, including the states of Alaska and Hawaii, with a sample of 2,277 adults, 18 years of age or older, contacted during the period July 5-10, 1988. Question was asked only of respondents whose telephone numbers end in 1, 3, 5, or 7: Original Print source does not show the percentage of these respondents with respect to the total sample.)*

VI. NOMENCLATURE

Prefer African-American or Black?

April 1991/February 1989

"Which would you prefer as a name for your race?" (Asked only of blacks—percentage of the sample is not provided by the print source)

	April 1991[1]	Feb. 1989[2]
Black	48 %	61 %
African-American	39	26

[1]*Time/CNN Poll conducted by Yankelovich, Clancy & Shulman. (The results of the survey are based on telephone interviews with 504 black adults, 18 and older, contacted during the period April 24-29, 1991. "Not sure" responses omitted—Error=4.5%.)*

[2]*Time Magazine Poll. February 1989. ("Not sure" responses omitted.)*

Is Nomenclature an Issue

July 1990

"When someone refers to your race, do you prefer to be referred to as black, African-American, or some other term?" (Asked only of black registered voters--14% of the total sample)

Black	59%
African-American	25
Some other term	8
Not sure	8

"Among the people you know, has there been much debate over this question of referring to blacks as African-Americans, or not?" (Asked only of black registered voters--14% of the total sample)

Yes	27 %
No	70
Not sure	3

The NBC News/Wall Street Journal Poll. (The results of the survey are based on telephone interviews with a national sample of 1,555 registered voters, 18 and older, contacted during the period July 6-10, 1990.)

APPENDIX

GUIDELINES FOR INTERPRETING PUBLIC OPINION POLLS

Poll results are always subject to error. Some errors can be attributed to sampling design and some are a result of nonsampling error — such as error in interpretation by either the pollsters or commentators, question wording, etc.

There are several reasons for exercising care in interpreting the results of any public opinion poll. The results of a single survey may be biased because of the timing of the study. Comparisons among the results of various polls may lead to faulty conclusions due to differences in question-wording, question order, the groups surveyed and the methods used by the various research firms. In addition, all polls and surveys based on samples of respondents are subject to error.

Sampling Errors

The results of sample surveys of the public are all subject to sampling error. Sampling error (best thought of as "uncertainty" rather than "mistake") is the potential for inaccuracy introduced because the survey only includes a fraction of the population studied. In general, larger samples mean smaller errors. However, the benefits derived from reducing the margin of error by one or two percentage points is usually not cost-effective. The margin of error in this report is plus or minus three percent unless otherwise noted. Keep in mind that the margin of error is applicable only for results based on the total sample; therefore, it will be difficult to make judgments on subgroups (such as blacks, union members, etc.) as the margin of error will be greater.

Who Was Polled?

One should always look at the population that was surveyed. Did the polling organization seek opinions from registered voters, likely voters, all adults, certain religious groups, certain age groups, etc.? Differences in the results from similar questions may occur because different populations are surveyed. For example, asking the same question of a sample of "registered voters" and of a sample of "likely voters" may produce widely different results because each sample is representative of a different population grouping. Some polling organizations may not call back hard-to-reach people or may not attempt to persuade respondents who initially refuse to be interviewed to change their minds. These poll results can be expected to show findings that differ from the results of polls conducted with more stringent methods. The reason is that some kinds of people are harder to reach, and they may behave differently from others. A New York Times/CBS News Poll conducted in September 1988 found that of registered voters reached on the first call, only 37 percent were men; with follow ups added, that proportion rose sharply.[6]

The Method of Contact

Using different methods of data collection (e.g., telephone interviewing and in-person interviewing) with exactly the same questions may produce different results as well. Frequently, surveys are taken by telephone interviews because they are more cost-effective. Even though polling organizations may make adjustments, this may still mean an underrepresentation of citizens from the lowest economic levels.[7]

Nonsampling Errors

Question Wording and Placement

A slight variation in the wording of a question may have a major impact on the results. This makes comparisons of the results of different surveys over a period of time more of a problem. Surveys only measure the response of the public to specific questions. Therefore, any variations might give the appearance that attitudes had "changed" when no such change had occurred. *Any* change in wording may mean that the survey is actually measuring something different from a previous survey on the same subject. According to William Schneider, a political analyst with the American Enterprise Institute for Public Policy Research, "every word, every modifier, every stipulation and every condition can make a difference."[8] For example, asking people about "aid to the needy" prompts a very different response than if you ask them about "welfare".

Question wording can have a pronounced effect on the responses given to policy questions, in which people do not have crystallized opinions. Questions on topics that arouse complex emotions, like abortion, or questions on remote topics like foreign policy are especially sensitive to the wording in questions."[9] Sometimes people react to the qualitative symbols and images presented in the

---

[6] Kagay, Michael R. In Judging Polls, What Counts Is When and How Who is Asked What. *The New York Times*, Sept. 12, 1988. p. A6.

[7] Germond, *To Understand Polls.*

[8] Jaroslovsky, Rich. What's On Your Mind, America? *Psychology Today*, July/August 1988. p. 56, 58.

[9] Kagay, In Judging Polls, p. A6.

questions (such as images of needy children, taxes, etc.) rather than on the basis of deeply held conviction.[10]

Question order can also alter results markedly. For example, suppose a polling agency develops a survey to measure a particular political leader's popularity. Then imagine that the pollster interviews a respondent who is generally unhappy with his/her personal financial status and the country's economic situation. In such a case, if the question about the political leader's popularity is asked after a series of questions about the economy and the respondent's financial situation, the leader's popularity rating would generally be lower than if the popularity question had been asked first. From this example, we can see that question order can alter the context within which the question is answered.[11]

Effects of Timing

The results of any single survey are based on interviews conducted during a short period of time, and events may cause public attitudes to change quite quickly and dramatically. Poll results are often skewed by news coverage. An empirical study by Shanto Iyengar and Donald R. Kinder showed that "television news . . . is a most powerful force determining what springs to the citizen's mind and what does not. By priming certain aspects of national life while ignoring others, television news sets the terms by which political judgments are rendered and political choices made."[12]

While a single survey may record attitudes at a moment in time, it cannot measure change. A review of the results of many surveys conducted over a period of time may provide a clearer picture of the stability or instability of public attitudes.

---

[10] Erikson, et al., *American Public Opinion*, p. 51-53.

[11] Asher, Herbert. *Polling and the Public: What Every Citizen Should Know*. Washington, Congressional Quarterly Inc., 1988. p. 46.

[12] Iyengar, Shanto, and Donald R. Kinder. *News That Matters: Television and American Opinion*. Chicago, The University of Chicago Press, 1987. p. 4.

Non-Attitudes And Interviewer Effects In Public Opinion Polling

Whenever possible, analysis of public opinion surveys should examine the extent of civic inattentiveness and the problems this creates for the proper interpretation of findings from opinion surveys.[13] Philip Converse, one of the early experts in the area of public opinion, estimated that less than 20 percent of the adult population holds meaningful opinions on more abstract or remote issues.[14] Numerous panel studies[15] have shown that people's attitudes on various issues over time are inconsistent.[16] Inconsistency is sometimes a result of true opinion conversion by individuals on a particular subject over time. However, often people's responses in panel studies are inconsistent because they lacked strong conviction or they responded to the question even though they did not have well formed attitudes on the topic.[17] The latter is often referred to as "nonattitudes." One way to minimize the extent of non-attitudes in survey responses is for polling organizations to include filter questions in the survey in order to find out whether or not individuals truly have an opinion on a particular issue. For example, a polling agency might ask the respondent if he knows enough about X to offer an opinion. If the respondent says yes, then the pollster could proceed with the question about X. Another way to reduce nonattitude responses is for the polling agency to ask more open-ended questions. Open-ended questions are ones in which a set response is not provided. They are used less frequently because they are difficult to code and they greatly increase the costs of a survey.

Since most survey questions are not accompanied by a filter and are not open-ended, analysts should be aware that many sociological factors can impair a poll's accuracy. Since many people do not want to appear uninformed when

---

[13] Erikson, et al., *American Public Opinion*. p. 40.

[14] Converse, Philip E. *The Nature of Belief Systems in Mass Publics*, In: Apter, David (ed.). *Ideology and Discontent*. New York, Free Press of Glencoe, 1964. p. 238-245; and Erikson, *American Public Opinion*. p. 49.

[15] Panel studies are those in which the same individuals are interviewed on the same subject more than once. They are useful in determining the volatility of public opinion on particular issues and/or candidates.

[16] Converse, Philip E. *Attitudes and Nonattitudes: Continuation of a Dialogue*. In: Tufte, Edward (ed.), *The Quantitative Analysis of Social Problems*. Reading, Mass., Addison-Wesley, 1970; Taylor, Marylee C. The Black-and-White Model of Attitude Stability: A Latent Class Examination of Opinion and Nonopinion in the American Public. *American Journal of Sociology*, v. 89, Sept. 1983. p. 373-401; and Norpoth, Helmut, and Milton Lodge. The Difference Between Attitudes and Nonattitudes in the Mass Public: Just Measurement? *American Journal of Political Science*, v. 29, May 1985. p. 291-307.

[17] Asher, *Polling and the Public*, p. 11.

they are approached by a pollster, many individuals will respond to a question even when they have not given the issue prior thought. Such responses are referred to as the "doorstep variety."[18] An example of the magnitude of this problem is exemplified in a 1980 study of the greater Cincinnati area which included a fictitious item in a survey:

> Respondents were presented with the following item about the nonexistent Public Affairs Act: "Some people say that the 1975 Public Affairs Act should be repealed. Do you agree or disagree with this idea?" Fully a third of the respondents offered an opinion on this version of the question.[19]

In short, the more remote the issue, the greater the chance that a larger share of the responses will be of the "doorstep variety." This is encouraged by the survey question's lack of any kind of a filter. If the question included a filter such as, " do you agree, disagree or have no opinion," then the results would be different than if a "no opinion" response has to be volunteered. The percentage of people claiming "no opinion" will be lower if the "no opinion" option is not given within the question.[20]

There is also what researchers call the "courtesy bias," i.e., people interviewed want to be liked and to give agreeable answers. They want to appear intelligent and often want their responses to be socially desirable.[21]

Furthermore, when people do not have a definite opinion on a subject, there is a tendency to agree. This is referred to as "response acquiescence."[22] An interviewer may unwittingly--or intentionally--obtain certain answers merely by smiling strategically.

---

[18] Ibid., p. 44.

[19] Asher, *Polling and the Public*. p. 22.

[20] Erikson, et al., *American Public Opinion*, p. 45.

[21] Yost, Barbara. Pollsters Struggle to Keep Up. *The Phoenix Gazette*, May 1, 1984.

[22] Erikson, et. al., *American Public Opinion*, p. 54.

HOW INFORMED IS THE AMERICAN PUBLIC?

Many Americans are arguably not very attentive observers of the political world. The typical citizen may have little political information at his or her disposal.[23] A recent survey of 18-44 year olds for *Rolling Stone* magazine conducted by Peter D. Hart Research Associates showed that only one in three said they followed the news regularly; 45 percent of those surveyed said that politics was either "not very important" or "not at all important" in their lives.[24] Many Americans do not follow current events closely enough to develop concrete opinions on topical political issues. Although political events can attract near-universal attention if they contain the necessary elements of human interest and drama, complicated political events or issues often get ignored by much of the general public.[25] Consequently, many Americans may *not* be able to offer informed opinions on specific government proposals.

However, the lack of an informed opinions on specific measures does not mean that individuals have no opinion on the subject, that they do not care about the broader issue, or that they may not vigorously oppose or support a specific policy. It may be that if an individual were provided with more information, he or she would then offer an informed opinion. In the final analysis, public opinion polls offer a picture of what is on the public's mind at a given point in time. Since this picture can sometimes appear muddled, users of public opinion must exercise care in drawing conclusions from poll results.

---

[23] Ibid., p. 40.

[24] Greider, William. Portrait of a Generation: The Rolling Stone Survey. *Rolling Stone*, Apr. 7, 1988. p. 53.

[25] Erikson, et al., *American Public Opinion*, p. 41.

SUBJECT INDEX